Stages on the Way

Also available:

Cloth for the Cradle

Worship resources and readings for Advent, Christmas, & Epiphany

G-5110

Stages on the Way

Worship resources and readings for Lent, Holy Week and Easter

Iona Community
The Wild Goose Worship Group

GIA Publications, Inc.
Chicago

ISBN 1-57999-076-2

Copyright © 2000, 1998 Wild Goose Resource Group

Front cover: Graham Maule © 2000, 1998 Wild Goose Resource Group

Published and distributed in North America by
GIA Publications, Inc.
7404 S. Mason Ave., Chicago, IL 60638
www.giamusic.com
1.800.GIA.1358 or 708.496.3800

**The Wild Goose is a Celtic symbol of the Holy Spirit.
It is the trademark of Wild Goose Publications.**

The Readings for the Seasons listed towards the end of this book are
reproduced from *The Revised Common Lectionary* (adapted). Copyright © 1992
by the Consultation on Common Texts (CCT), PO Box 840, Room 381,
Nashville TN 37202-0840, USA. Used with permission from CCT.

Extracts which appear from *The Good News Bible, The New English Bible* and
The Revised English Bible are used with permission.

Contents

Introduction

Like CLOTH FOR THE CRADLE, the first in this series of WGWG worship resource books, STAGES ON THE WAY is a book of bits.

You will not find here a complete liturgy or order of service. Nor will you find prayers or collects for all the Sundays in Lent. Nor an entire Palm Sunday service or Easter Vigil. What you will find are bits, fragments, resources for shaping the worship of God's people during the seasons of Lent, Holy Week and Easter.

This is the way this series of books has evolved because this is the way the Wild Goose Worship Group works – as enablers of what might be rather than as authors of what cannot be repeated.

The material contained here has been in circulation for between one and fifteen years. Everything has been through our mouths and the mouths of other people and amended according to experience or suggestions. While few of the prayers or liturgical responses have been published before, some of the scripts have.

Some of the material evolved for use in our own group worship, some at LAST NIGHT OUT (our monthly adult event in Glasgow), some for Holy Week worship services we have been asked to lead in our home city. All of these have provided fertile ground, but the major crop of material has grown out of the various times over the years we have shared in leading the program on Iona during Holy Week.

There the emphasis has been to enable participants to walk with Christ, to feel the range of emotions provoked by the twists and turns of his Passion and to discover echoes and empathies in their own lives: in short, to experience Easter. Not uncoincidentally, EXPERIENCING EASTER is the very title by which that annual event on Iona is known.

STAGES ON THE WAY attempts to enable the same. Its title is inspired by a characteristic of these liturgical seasons. All are marked by a series of *progressions*. The weeks of Lent are a progression from the countryside to the city; despite starting and ending with a shout, the seven days from Palm Sunday to Easter Day traverse a whole range of emotions. Through the resurrection appearances to Christ's ascension, the believers progress through fear to courage, from private suspicion to public testimony, from a scattered band of loners and losers to a tightly knit community of faith.

In the Church's worship as it celebrates all of these stages, it is helpful if people can see and feel these progressions; so a sensitivity as to how this might happen should be developed.

How can this kind of thing begin to be creatively enabled? A few perhaps fairly obvious pointers may be mentioned here.

At Christmas, we have no difficulty in decorating our churches, but during Holy Week and Easter, we are more reticent and less lavish. This is partly because Lent is an ascetic season and many traditions discourage flowers in church during this time; but there are several possibilities which need not transgress denominational sensitivities, and we offer some here. These are primarily drawn from experiences in Glasgow or on Iona; what happens in one venue is not directly transportable to another, so these suggestions for symbolic action are offered not for replication, but for modification. GOOD FRIDAY, one example of this type of material, can be found on page 125.

Holy Week and Easter are the times which offer Jesus' people the greatest possibility of understanding exactly what belonging to his kingdom and being recipients of his love might really mean. Perhaps, unsurprisingly, they are also the times which offer the greatest possibility of discovering what his followers can do and be for him, in their lives, today.

We hope this book of bits, in the sensitive hands of worship planners and leaders, of both lay and clerical hues, may aid God's people in this deepening of their experience of Easter and of God.

Alison Adam
Graham Maule
for the Wild Goose Worship Group

Using this book

There are six basic types of material in the book, each of which is indicated by a recurrent symbol.

△ **Liturgical material**, often sets of shared responses for use of aleader and congregation.

○ **Prayers**, which may be read by one person, with the occasional option of a congregational spoken or sung response.

| **Readings**, which may be poems or monologues, normally requiring one reader.

∨ **Meditations**, which will require one or more voices and may be accompanied by action.

□ **Scripts**, which may be read by two or more people and which lend themselves to dramatic presentation.

↑ **Symbolic actions**, which enable the congregation to be actively engaged in the worship by physically moving around the building.

The material is arranged chronologically, roughly complementing the progress of the readings for the seasons. This, however, does not mean that a set of responses for Lent would necessarily be inappropriate for Holy Week. There is room for interchange.

It is envisaged that worship leaders will select materials from the book and incorporate them into acts of worship, rather than make a liturgy simply out of what is found here. Or it may be that in some of these resources leaders will see models which they might use to help devise their own materials.

However, a word might be offered with respect to the different types of material found here.

Liturgical material is, by and large, meant to be shared by the whole congregation. Therefore, these items should be printed or photocopied onto service sheets.

We strongly advise people to use the same set of responses throughout the season of Lent, changing them when Holy Week and then Easter come along. It is tedious to congregations to be asked to repeat a different set of words every Sunday. Whether the responses are used at the beginning or end of worship, or precede or follow scripture readings, is at the user's discretion.

Prayers need not be seen by everyone. They are meant to be read in the hearing of the congregation. They should therefore be rehearsed aloud in advance of worship, so that all the words feel comfortable in the reader's mouth. To give someone a prayer at the last minute or to glance at the prayer the minute before you read it is insulting to God to whom the worship is offered and also to God's people on behalf of whom the prayer is said. Use of silence and sung or spoken congregational responses is encouraged where appropriate.

Readings may be suitable for some folk and not for others. As with prayers, adequate rehearsal is required both in private and in the space where the reading will be delivered. The best readers are not those with contrived accents or drama school diplomas, but people who are prepared to be, for the moment, the mouth of God (when reading Scripture) or the representative of one of God's people (when reading a monologue). If the story or the poem or the words have gone through an individual's system several times, they will come out with conviction. If they have not done the rounds of his or her body, they will remain on the page.

While readings will usually be delivered facing a congregation, **meditations** need not happen in the same way. It has been our experience that people can engage imaginatively with meditative readings when they do not face the reader, but rather when the voice or voices come from the side or back as appropriate.

The feeling of voices coming from around cannot happen when microphones and amplifiers are used. These channel all sound through the speakers, irrespective of where the reader is standing. A natural acoustic is therefore preferable, and most buildings can be so used if the congregation or audience sit together towards the front and if readers speak with their backs to a solid wall which becomes a sounding board.

Of course, the politically correct lobby will remind us that there are hard-of- hearing people in church. There are also people of limited mobility who cannot take part in every symbolic action, as there are people with restricted vision who cannot see what is happening at the front.

Those who lobby for people with one disadvantage cannot rule or amend everything that happens in worship. To allow for a minimal degree of temporary discomfort is to demonstrate that kind of hospitality to others, which is central to the Christian faith.

Scripts, like readings, do not require gifted performers. Many of the dialogues included here can simply be read by people standing in appropriate parts of the worship space which will not necessarily be at the front of, but may be in the midst of or around the periphery of, the seated congregation. For people who are keen to provide some kind of continuous narrative on Jesus' Passion throughout Holy Week, there are a number of monologues and dialogues included in this collection. These may be complemented by appropriate songs or chants to tell the story.

Symbolic actions should primarily be optional rather than obligatory. Not everyone feels easy about lighting a candle, or moving from their seat to a distant part of the church. This should be respected. People are usually quite happy for others to engage in such actions as long as they are not personally compelled. When symbolic action is taking place, it is essential that any visuals used or created can be seen.

Just as we would like to encourage those who have purchased this book for its liturgical material to consider using some meditations or scripts, so we would encourage those who favor the latter also to try the former. There are too many false presumptions made about congregations by those who claim to "know what they can take." It has consistently surprised us to see high church Anglo Catholics, who seem riveted to the Prayer Book, relaxing when a humorous dialogue is employed sensitively and in the right place, just as it has amused us to see diehard Protestants warm at the prospect of doing the "papish" thing of lighting a candle.

Finally, we encourage users of this material to think about the space in which it is used. Up to a third of the difficulties people encounter in trying something new in worship has to do with the building in which they meet, yet architecture and seating are often last on our list of things to be considered.

When people sit far apart, not only will they find it difficult to sing, they will find it awkward to laugh and difficult to listen. There is something enabling about being *part* of a congregation as distinct from being *apart* from the congregation. Of course, there is a place for personal piety, but the corporate worship of God's people should not always be held ransom to the needs of individuals to have their own sacred space. Jesus advised such people to use their closet.

Because most lay people do not spend their time prancing about chancels or speaking from lecterns, the more comfortable leaders can feel, in moving around the building or hearing their voice sound in it, the better.

There are lots of other things we would like to say, but too many words of advice might be more of a hindrance than a help.

We therefore encourage you to enjoy using the material in the book.

Reproducing the material

Unless otherwise indicated, the material in this book is copyrighted by the Wild Goose Resource Group, Iona Community. GIA Publications, Inc., is the exclusive North American distributor.

Permission is granted to reproduce portions of this book for non-commercial purposes for use by the congregation, so long as copies of this book are purchased for each of the readers. Please indicate the copyright source as follows:

If wishing to reproduce any of the material for commercial purposes (e.g., inclusion in a book or recording for sale, or workshop material for which a fee is to be charged), permission must be sought in writing from GIA Publications, Inc., 7404 S. Mason Ave., Chicago, IL 60638. Fax: (708) 496-3828. E-mail: custserv@giamusic.com.

△ Everything happens
Lent responses 1

This set of responses, adapted from Ecclesiastes 3, is particularly appropriate for use at the beginning of Lent.

Leader: Everything that happens on earth
happens at the time God chooses.

Women: God sets the time for birth and the time for death,
Men: the time for sorrow and the time for joy,

Women: the time for tearing and the time for mending,
Men: the time for scattering and the time for gathering,

Women: the time for seeking and the time for losing,
Men: the time for keeping silence and the time for speaking.

Leader: Everything that happens on earth
ALL: HAPPENS AT THE TIME GOD CHOOSES.

I am giving you me
Lent meditation 1

This meditation may be used at the beginning of Lent, on Ash Wednesday. The sung response JESUS CHRIST, SON OF GOD AMONG US (from the THERE IS ONE AMONG US collection) may be sung continuously at the end. There are three readers. A and B should be positioned at the front of the congregation, to the left and right; C, who speaks the words of Jesus, should speak from the back.

Personnel: **A**
B
C (Jesus)

A: I
B: I

A: I am
B: I am

A: I am giving
B: I am giving

A: I am giving you
B: I am giving you

A: I am giving you me
B: I am giving you me

A: I am giving you me, Lord.
B: I am giving you me, Lord.

B: I am giving you me
in the twinkle of my eye
and the sadness of my sighing;
in the laughter of my heart
and the tears of my soul;
in the rhythms of my feet
and the silence of my listening.

I am giving you me, Lord.

A: I am giving you me
in the promises I keep
and the insults that I pardon;
in the good news that I share
and the confidences I protect;
in the remembering of gracious things
and the forgetting of forgiven sins.

I am giving you me, Lord.

B: I am giving you me
in the young ones I kneel beside
and the old ones I sit with;
in the unborn ones I pray for
and the dying ones I pray with;
in the bright ones I wave to
and the hurting ones I touch.

I am giving you me, Lord.

A: I am giving you me
in the meant song,
in the quiet pause,
in the special moment,
in the nod of my life to your will
and still,
I am giving you me
in the stuttered prayer
and the lingering doubt
and the dry days of the spirit
and the contradicted hopes.

I am giving you me, Lord.

C: I
I am
I am giving
I am giving you
I am giving you me
I am giving you me, my brothers and sisters.

I am giving you me
in the beauty of the earth
and the ugliness of a wooden cross;
in the fullness of four seasons

and the emptiness of a garden tomb;
in the warmth of the weak
and the rejection of the mighty;
in the company of God's people
and the solitude of a place apart;

and sometimes,
when a stone wall confronts you,
I am giving you me,
praying on the other side:
    Father,
    may the love you have for me
    be in them,
    so that I may also
    be in them
    and they in us.

Your thoughts are not our thoughts
Lent prayer 1

This responsive prayer is particularly appropriate for use at the beginning of Lent on Ash Wednesday.

Leader: Glorious God,
your thoughts are not our thoughts,
neither are your ways our ways.

You look at the ugliest soul
and see, still unstirred,
the wings of an angel.

ALL: WE SCAN THE FINEST OF OUR NEIGHBORS,
ANXIOUS TO FIND THE FLAW.

Leader: You view time in the context of eternity,
and so find a place for waiting, for yearning,
even for suffering, even for dying.

ALL: WE DEMAND INSTANT RESULTS;
AND LOOK FOR TOMORROW BEFORE SAVORING
TODAY.

Leader: You know that only one who suffers
can ultimately save,
that is why you walk the way of the cross.

ALL: WE FEAR THAT VULNERABILITY
WHICH DEFIES OUR POWER;
AND SO WE CRY FOR CRUCIFIXION.

Leader: Your thoughts are not our thoughts,
ALL: NEITHER ARE YOUR WAYS OUR WAYS.

Leader: And yet we know
that your way is the ladder to heaven,
while, left to our own devices,
our ways slope downwards to hell.
But we are here,
not to have our worst confirmed,
but to have our best liberated.

ALL: So we pray,
FORGIVE IN US WHAT HAS GONE WRONG,
REPAIR IN US WHAT IS WASTED,
REVEAL IN US WHAT IS GOOD.

Leader: And nourish us with better food
than we could ever purchase:
your word,
your love,
your inspiration,
your daily bread for our life's journey,
in the company of Jesus Christ, our Lord.

ALL: AMEN.

Before you, Jesus Christ
Lent prayer 2

*Another prayer appropriate for Ash Wednesday, the response here
(Lord, Have Mercy/ CHRIST HAVE MERCY) may be replaced by a sung
KYRIE ELEISON.*

Leader:	Before you, Jesus Christ, we admit how and where we have underestimated our influence, letting our words or silences hurt, abusing trust, betraying confidences.
ALL:	Lord, have mercy; CHRIST, HAVE MERCY.
Leader:	We admit how and where we have made a show of our religion, attracting more attention to us, and less to you.
ALL:	Lord, have mercy; CHRIST, HAVE MERCY.
Leader:	We admit to where in our lives a vague interest has become a dangerous passion, and we are not sure what to do or whether we are still in control.
ALL:	Lord, have mercy; CHRIST, HAVE MERCY.
Leader:	Lord Jesus Christ, if we have looked or longed for an easier gospel, a lighter cross, a less demanding savior, then turn our eyes and avert our longing

from what we want to choose
to the one who has chosen us.

Forgive our unfaithfulness,
and, for our better living,
give us not the remedy we desire tomorrow,
but the grace you offer today.

We ask this for your love's sake.
AMEN.

☐ A very reasonable man
Lent script 1

This is a version of the Temptation story in Luke 4; essentially, a reflection has been added after each of the Devil's invitations to Jesus, and the whole script then divided into four voices: two narrators, Jesus and the Devil. The only character who need appear in this script is the Devil. He/she should look and sound like a trustworthy estate agent showing interested parties a new house. At the end, he/she has to change his/her mode of dress in some way, perhaps putting on an overcoat or perhaps a hat and scarf. Jesus can appear in person or be represented in voice alone. The two narrators should not be prominent, but if seen, Narrator A should always face the congregation and Narrator B should sit facing away from them, turning around only to speak.

Few props are needed: a table (or the altar/communion table could be used) with several large stones on it or near it and a dossier file for the Devil in which he/she can carry his/her script and relate to it for scriptural quotations in an evident way.

The Devil speaks from three positions – the table, a high point in the building (a pulpit, gallery or top-raked pew), and a prominent position near a window from which he/she can see the world.

A suitable chant (e.g., BLESS THE LORD , MY SOUL from Taizé or any short Kyrie) should be sung to intersperse the episodes while the Devil moves.

Personnel: **Narrator A**
Narrator B
Devil
Jesus

Narrator A: It happened,
that after Jesus had been baptized,
and while he was full of the Holy Spirit,
he was led, by the Spirit, into the desert.
There he remained for forty days and forty nights,
during which time he ate nothing,

but was tempted by the Devil.

(Song or chant; the Devil enters, looks about and moves to the table)

Narrator B: Now the Devil knew the ways
and the will of God intimately.
He had been long used to alluring people
by the subtlest of means.

The Devil was also a very compassionate man.
He recognized hunger when he saw it,
and showed concern for its victim by saying,

Devil: Jesus,
you're hungry ...
and you're God's Son.
God's Son doesn't need to be famished.

Look,
here are some stones.
They could be loaves.
Your word could change them.

Go on, change them.

Narrator A: But Jesus answered,

Jesus: The Scripture says,
"Man cannot live by bread alone,
 but needs every word that God speaks."

(Song or chant; the Devil changes position)

Narrator A: The Devil then took Jesus to Jerusalem,
the Holy City.
He brought him to the temple
and set him on its highest point.

Narrator B: Now the Devil was a very knowledgeable man.
He knew the scriptures.
He could quote them
to show his familiarity with God.
So he said,

Devil: Jesus,
you are God's Son,
and this is God's holy place.

Below are those who wait to believe,
who want to believe,
but need a sign to convince them.

So, why not – seeing as you are God's Son –
why not throw yourself down.
Remember what the Scripture says –
the Holy Scripture –

(Consults file)

Psalm 91, verses 11 and 12 to be precise,
   "God will give orders to his angels about you;
   they will hold you up with their hands,
   so that not even your feet
   will be hurt on the stones."

Narrator A: Jesus answered,

Jesus: The Scripture also says,
"Do not put the Lord your God to the test."

(Song or chant; the Devil changes position)

Narrator A: Then the Devil took Jesus to a very high mountain.
He showed him all the kingdoms of the world
in all their greatness.

Narrator B: Now the Devil was a very reasonable man.
He realized the grasp he had over people
worldwide.
He realized also
how Jesus wanted all creation to know him as Lord.
So he made a proposal, a contract,
whereby Jesus could have all his heart desired.

Devil: Jesus,
oh, my friend Jesus,
all that I have, I would give to you.
All that you want should be,
                    could be, yours.
Just bend the knee,
and worship me.

Narrator A: Jesus answered,

Jesus: Go away, Satan.
The Scripture says,
"Worship the Lord your God
 and serve only him."

*(Song or chant; the Devil exits in order to change
 clothes slightly; he/she reappears while Narrator B
 speaks)*

Narrator A: Jesus was left alone,
and angels came to help him.

Narrator B: *(The Devil re-enters, looking around at people as
he/she walks around)*

The Devil went elsewhere
to walk the earth
as a very compassionate,
              knowledgeable
                and reasonable man.

And still,
the Prince of Hell
and Master of Disguises,
appears, incognito,
as an angel of light.

*(The Devil now hums the song or chant previously
used, and exits)*

Because you were tempted
Lent intercessions 1

Each section of this prayer is best interspersed with a short silence, followed by a sung response, such as the KYRIE (BRIDGET) from the THERE IS ONE AMONG US collection. Alternatively, the words (in the Greek or in English, "Lord, have mercy") may be spoken by all. In that case, the leader should say the words first with the people repeating them.

Leader: Lord Jesus Christ,
we pray to you
because you were tempted like us,
in all things,
yet did not submit;

because you have promised
to come to the help of those who,
in every age, are put to the test;

and because we are not exempt
from the subtle attraction
of what is wrong and what is evil,
therefore we pray to you.

(Silence then KYRIE)

Leader: We call you
to where, in our lives,
we exploit our abilities purely for personal gain,
and let the human gifts,
which were meant to illuminate the world,
light up no more than our own vanity.

(Silence then KYRIE)

Leader: We call you
to where, in our lives,
we have made a show of our religion

and made faith a means of attracting to us,
at the cost of distracting from you.

(Silence then KYRIE)

Leader: We call you
to where, in our lives,
another god, more to our liking,
is the object of our fawning,

the recipient of our time,
        of our attention,
        of our worship.

(Silence then KYRIE)

Leader: For it is in these places in our lives
that we threaten to desert you,
the one who has chosen us
and who,
in the wilderness,
at the Temple
and on the mountaintop
showed there was a better way.

So we turn
from our seeking after selfish comfort,
we turn
from our inclination to false piety,
we turn
from our preference for petty loyalties.

From these we avert our gaze,
turning our faces towards you,
Jesus Christ, our Lord.
AMEN.

Lord, help us to say no
Lent meditation 2

This meditation focuses on the many apparently unimportant choices we have to face, which nevertheless may significantly affect our discipleship to Jesus. As such, it may be useful on the first Sunday of Lent.

It may be preferable to have seven readers, one for each section, but at least two are needed, who alternate. Unlike many others, this meditation is best listened to with eyes open, as it has a visual dimension.

The lighting in the worship area should be dimmed. A total of 12 candles and a cross are needed. After each section of the meditation, the reader who has just read blows out a candle, then places a lit candle at the cross (which should be centrally located).

Personnel: **A**
B

A: When the advertisements offer us everything,
if only we have the money;
and you offer everything
If only we do without,
Lord, help us to say "no";

(Blows out candle)

help us to say "yes."

(Places lit candle at the cross)

B: When the easier way to succeed
means we lose our integrity,
but the harder way,
means we lose our pride,
Lord, help us to say "no";

(Blows out candle)

help us to say "yes."

(Places lit candle at the cross)

A: When the Church wants us to conform
and be nice,
and you want us to rebel
and be real,
Lord, help us to say "no";

(Blows out candle)

help us to say "yes."

(Places lit candle at the cross)

B: When our friends don't respect
what we count as important,
and we feel like giving in,
just to save face,
Lord, help us to say "no";

(Blows out candle)

help us to say "yes."

(Places lit candle at the cross)

A: When we feel you have let us down
and we want to leave you,
but we know we left you behind
before we ever started,
Lord, help us to say "no";

(Blows out candle)

help us to say "yes."

(Places lit candle at the cross)

B: When we have come to a crossroads
and we don't know where to turn,
but we know that to stand still
is the greater danger,
Lord, help us to say "no";

(Blows out candle)

help us to say "yes."

(Places lit candle at the cross)

A: Jesus Christ, the Son of God,
      who has been preached among you
      is not one who is "yes" and "no."
      On the contrary,
      he is God's "yes";
      for it is he who is the "yes"
      to all God's promises.

Lord Jesus Christ, you refused
Lent prayer 3

A: Lord Jesus Christ,
you refused to turn stones into bread.
Save us from using our power,
however little,
to satisfy the demands of selfishness
in the face of the needs of others.

B: Lord Jesus Christ,
you refused to leap from the temple top.
Save us from displaying our skills,
however modest,
to win instant popularity
in the face of nobler calls on our abilities.

C: Lord Jesus Christ,
you refused to bend the knee to a false god.
Save us from offering our devotion,
however weak,
to cheap or easy religion
in the face of the harder path
on which you bid us to follow you.

A: Savior of the World,
you saw Satan masquerading as an angel of light
and shunned him.
Give us wisdom
to discern behind each subtle temptation
the ploy of the prince of darkness;
and in the face of all that is hellishly attractive,
help us to choose the will of God.
AMEN.

From Bethlehem to Nazareth
Lent responses 2

These responses are appropriate for the second Sunday in Lent, but may also be used during Holy Week.

Leader: From Bethlehem to Nazareth,
from Jordan to Jericho,
from Bethany to Jerusalem,
from then to now,
ALL: COME, LORD JESUS.

Leader: To heal the sick,
to mend the broken-hearted,
to comfort the disturbed,
to disturb the comfortable,
to cleanse the temple,
to liberate faith from convention,
ALL: COME, LORD JESUS.

Leader: To carry the cross,
to lead the way,
to shoulder the sin of the world
and take it away,
ALL: COME, LORD JESUS.

Leader: Today,
to this place,
to us,
ALL: COME, LORD JESUS.

The servant is coming
Lent responses 3

Based on Isaiah 52, this set of responses is suitable for the second Sunday of Lent, but may also be used towards the end of the season.

Leader: The servant is coming whom God upholds,
the chosen one in whom God delights.
ALL: ON HIM GOD'S SPIRIT FIRMLY RESTS,
BY HIM GOD'S JUSTICE WILL BE DONE.

Leader: He will not shout or raise his voice,
ALL: HE WILL NOT FALTER OR BE CRUSHED.

Leader: In him God's holy arm is bared,
ALL: THROUGH HIM GOD'S SURE SALVATION COMES.

Leader: Then let the watchers shout for joy
and let the wasted places sing:
ALL: NOW IS THE TIME FOR DELIVERANCE!
NOW EARTH'S REDEEMER HAS COME!

The servant
Lent reading 1

The beautiful Scottish melody to the tune AE FOND KISS fits these words perfectly. However, they can be read equally effectively as a poem. A paraphrase of the passage in Isaiah 53 which identifies God's "suffering servant," it is especially appropriate for the second and third Sundays in Lent.

Who would ever have belicved it?
Who could ever have conceived it?
Who dared trace God's hand behind it
when a servant came among us?

Like a sapling in dry soil,
he was rooted in our presence;
lacking beauty, grace and splendor,
no one felt attracted to him.

We despised him, we disowned him,
though he clearly hurt and suffered:
we, believing he was worthless,
never turned our eyes towards him.

Yet it was the pain and torment
we deserved which he accepted,
while we reckoned his afflictions
must have come by heaven's instruction.

Though our sins let him be wounded,
though our cruelty left him beaten,
yet, through how and why he suffered,
God revealed our hope of healing.

We, like sheep despite our wisdom,
all had wandered from God's purpose;
and our due in pain and anger
God let fall on one among us.

(Repeat verse one to end)

No, Jesus, no!
Lent script 2

It was some time before Jesus' disciples fully realized who he really was and what were the implications of his mission. And as they moved towards Jerusalem, this realization probably grew hand in hand with their misgivings and fear of what was to come. This script imagines a conversation between a disciple and Jesus at that time.

The disciple should be at the front of the congregation, with Jesus positioned at the back.

Personnel: **Disciple**
Jesus

Disciple: *(Pacing backwards and forwards, as if in anguish)*

No, Jesus, no!

(Wheels around and directs speech to Jesus at the back)

Hardly three years ...
that's all we've known you,
long enough to know
not to want to keep you to ourselves,
long enough to know we share you,
but not to lose you.

No,
not the miracles ...
not the quieted storm,
not the fish that fed five thousand,
not the withered arms turning strong ...
these – all right, they're important –
but they're not why we follow you.

It's *you*.
You ... that's why we're here.
That's why this unsophisticated crew

of half-baked fishermen and non-events
trail behind you.

You said "Come."
And not knowing where or why,
we followed;
and now,
just when everything begins to fall into place,
just when our eyes are beginning
to recognize who you are,
you want to end it all.

Do you want to die, Jesus?
Or is it the heat?
Or has the pressure of the crowds
scared off your sanity?

Look, forget the Passover.
There'll be other years,
and besides,
we've all been before.
What do you say?

(Stands and stares at Jesus)

Jesus: We're going up to Jerusalem
and when we get there,
I'll be handed over to the chief priests and scribes.
They will sentence me to die
and hand me over to the Romans to be killed.
They will mock me
and spit on me
and flog me with their whips
and kill me;
but after three days
I will come back to life again.

(Disciple turns away from Jesus and exits)

Stages on the way
Lent script 3

These stages represent different aspects of Jesus' journey towards the cross as seen by a variety of bystanders. The nature of the building in which the script is used will, to some extent, dictate the way in which the words can best be communicated, but here are two examples of how it has been employed:

1) In a large inner-city parish, at morning worship, the seven readers were situated behind the congregation. This enabled those who were apprehensive about reading in a fairly dramatic manner to lose some of their nervousness. After each reader had finished, the organ played a solo line from one of the passion hymns such as WHEN I SURVEY THE WONDROUS CROSS. During the music the reader brought forward something which would be required for making a cross (nails, a hammer, a saw, rope, two large planks of wood) and left it in a central location.

2) At a large evening youth event in a contemporary church building, seven large posters were prepared which depicted the activities alluded to in the script. These were hung on the walls of the church, from the back, around one side towards the chancel where a wooden cross stood. Each poster had a spotlight (an anglepoise lamp) focused on it. The chant, MISERERE NOBIS/ Have mercy on us, Lord (from the LOVE FROM BELOW collection) was sung as the sanctuary lights dimmed. Then, one by one, the spotlights lit up the posters while the readers said the appropriate words. After each reading, the light was extinguished and the chant sung once. At the end, all eyes had moved from the back of the church to the cross at which time prayers were said.

It is important that, however the script is employed, the voices should sound natural. The range of characters represented allows for a good cross section of any congregation or group to be used.

A KYRIE ELEISON/ Lord, have mercy may be used instead of the MISERERE NOBIS suggested above; or alternatively a short piece of instrumental music may be played.

Personnel:	**Farmer**
	Pharisee
	Trader
	Priest
	Worshipper
	Judas
	Laborer

Farmer: You have it coming to you.

You cannot wander around the country
with a dozen vagrants,
some of whom can't speak properly,
and expect to be believed.

Your "disciples" ...
if you can call them that ...
are common.
And you,
with your stories
of lost coins and runaway children,
are far from sophisticated.

People want a Messiah,
not a former tradesman.
If you pretend to be one,
but are the other,
you must take the consequences.

(Sung response or music)

Pharisee: You have it coming to you!

There is a time for playing the fool.
There is a time for poking fun
at what is serious in politics and religion.
But there is a border line
between jesting and indiscretion,
which you obviously don't recognize.

Riding on a donkey,
with your starry-eyed friends
throwing the shirts off their backs
in front of you,
and doing this in "royal style" ...

that may be quite a laugh after dark,
when the streets are empty apart from drunk men.

But not,
not in the light of day
in the most sacred week of the year.

Those who do that
must be prepared for the consequences!

(Sung response or music)

Trader: You have it coming to you.

The police saw you,
the priests saw you,
the people saw you ...
and though they cheered
don't be deluded.

"The Temple is a house of prayer" –
who would disagree?
But if so,
why scatter pigeons and coins
all over the place?

Of course,
if it's sensationalism you're after,
you are going the right way about it.
You might say that people
are more important than sparrows.
But send holy doves scurrying into the air
and soon you'll discover what's really sacred.

(Sung response or music)

Priest: You have it coming to you!

The place of worship is not a laboratory.
It is not for experiments.
It is not for seeing how far you can go
before someone shouts, "No further!"

People sit still.
They listen to the Word.
They listen to the preaching.
They do not move,

44

nor were they ever meant to.
And certainly,
those who look the worst
never seek the limelight.

But you ...
you ask sick people to come forward.
And so they come,
with their withered arms and scabby faces,
lining up as if for a freak show or circus.

Healing?
Oh, there is a place for healing;
but not here!
Not here!

(Sung response or music)

Worshipper: You have it coming to you.

You are taking God
into the marketplace
without permission.

You sit with the unemployed
and pretend that God is there.
You kneel down beside a whore
and pretend that God is there.
You smile at soldiers, heathen soldiers,
and pretend that God loves them.
You cannot do this to God.
You cannot take him where you want to go.

Worse still –
you cannot say that he is there already ...
unless, of course,
you don't believe in the God we believe in ...
in which case, we have nothing to learn,
but plenty to teach you.

(Sung response or music)

Judas: You have it coming to you.

And I am going to help it happen.

Three years I've watched you,
listened to you,
copied you
and have been let down.

For at the moment
when you could have triumphed;
at the time
when you had the crowds
eating out of your hand;
whenever people were ready
for something big,
what do you do?

You chicken out;
away into the hills for a wander ...
slink down a side street,
say, "Enough ... enough ...
there will be another time!"

Well, the time is coming.
I am your stage manager
and I have negotiated my fee.

In a little while,
the eyes of all will be on you.
Then you'll show them who you are
and what you can do.

And afterwards,
my thirty pieces of silver
will buy a good carry-out
for yourself and the boys.

(Sung response or music)

Laborer: You have it coming to you.

You don't know it,
but this wood is for you.

Now, being a carpenter,
you could do lovely things with it ...
turn it,
dovetail it,
sand it down.

But we can't,
for we're not carpenters.
We're not even joiners.
We're just laborers,
earning money on the side.

But we've been told
to keep quiet about our business.

So, without giving anything away,
but seeing as you might be
who they say you are,
we'll let you know
that we're making something beautiful
for God.

Ha ha, ha ha.

Jerusalem, Jerusalem
Lent meditation 3

This meditation consists of biblical extracts (from passages in Jeremiah 8 & 9, Isaiah 16 and Luke 13) where God sheds tears. Appropriate for the third Sunday in Lent, it presents the situations of suffering which produce this emotional response in God. As an expression of the people's hurt, between each section, a KYRIE may be sung and, as that is done, one of three large candles (placed in visible locations) may be extinguished in turn. Then after each passage of Scripture, there is a silence.

A prayer of intercession might follow. It might be designed to have three sections with the petitions in each, focusing on the situations described in the three Scriptural passages.

Personnel: **Narrator**
              God
              Candle extinguisher (optional)

Narrator: Listen,
                 for this is the Lord speaking.
                 There are tears on God's cheeks
                 for the people who are suffering.

                 (Sung response, as the first candle is blown out)

God: I am crushed because my people are crushed.
                 I mourn.
                 I am completely dismayed.
                 Is there no medicine in the land?
                 Are there no doctors there?
                 Why, then, have my people not been healed?
                 I wish my head were a well of water
                 and my eyes a fountain of tears
                 so that I could cry day and night
                 for the suffering of my people.

                 (Silence)

Narrator: Listen,
for this is the Lord speaking.
There are tears on God's cheeks
for the people who are hungry.

(Sung response, as the second candle is blown out)

God: I weep for the vineyards
and I weep for the country.
My tears fall for the towns
where there is no harvest to make the people glad.
No one is happy now in the fertile fields;
no one shouts or sings in the vineyards,
no one tramps grapes to make wine;
the shouts of joy are ended,
my people hunger.

(Silence)

Narrator: Listen,
for this is the Lord speaking.
There are tears on Jesus' cheeks
for the people who miss the opportunities for

peace.

(Sung response, as the third candle is blown out)

God: Jerusalem, Jerusalem, you murder the prophets
and slaughter those God sends you.
If only you knew today the way that leads to peace,
but you cannot see it.
Therefore other people will destroy you
and not a stone will be left in its place.
This will happen because you did not recognize
the time when God came to save you.

(Silence)

Narrator: Listen,
for this is the Lord speaking.
There are tears on God's cheek:
tears for the callous
tears for the uncared for:

God: The wound of the daughter of my people
wounds me, too.

On the mountaintop
Lent prayer 4

Lord Jesus Christ,
on the mountaintop, Peter, James and John
looked upon the majesty of your glory,
and from the mystery of a cloud
heard a voice declaring you to be God's Son.

Though we do not live on mountaintops,
grant that we too may glimpse your glory.

In the mundane predictability of our lives
may there be for us moments
when sight gives way to insight,
and the paths of earth
become the road to heaven.
AMEN

Son of Mary, have mercy on us

Lent litany 1

Evoking the journey of Jesus and his disciples towards Jerusalem, this litany of confession is particularly useful in the latter Sundays in Lent.

Leader: Son of Mary,
ALL: HAVE MERCY ON US.

Leader: Carpenter of Nazareth,
ALL: HAVE MERCY ON US.

Leader: Healer of the sick,
ALL: HAVE MERCY ON US.

Leader: Bringer of good news,
ALL: HAVE MERCY ON US.

Leader: Savior of the poor,
ALL: HAVE MERCY ON US.

Leader: Disturber of the mighty,
ALL: HAVE MERCY ON US.

Leader: Contradicter of the smooth,
ALL: HAVE MERCY ON US.

Leader: Destroyer of false religion,
ALL: HAVE MERCY ON US.

Leader: You, who moves towards Jerusalem,
trailing hope and hell behind you,
ALL: HAVE MERCY ON US.

Leader: You, who calls us sister, mother, brother, friend
and who asks us to come with you,
ALL: HAVE MERCY ON US.

Where Christ walks
Lent responses 4

As well as being well suited to the third week in Lent, when suffering is the theme, this litany could be just as appropriately used on Good Friday.

Leader: Where Christ walks,
ALL: WE WILL FOLLOW.

Leader: Where Christ stumbles,
ALL: WE WILL STOP.

Leader: Where Christ cries,
ALL: WE WILL LISTEN.

Leader: Where Christ suffers,
ALL: WE WILL HURT.

Leader: When Christ dies,
ALL: WE WILL BOW OUR HEADS IN SORROW.

Leader: When Christ rises again in glory,
ALL: WE WILL SHARE HIS ENDLESS JOY.

Leader: There is no other way;
ALL: HE IS THE ONLY WAY.

In this world
Lent prayer 5

Lord God,
in this world where goodness and evil
continue to clash with each other,
instil in us, and in all your people,
   discernment to see what is right,
   faith to believe what is right,
   and courage to do what is right.

Keep us aware of the subtlety of sin,
and preserve us, body, mind and soul,
through the power of your Holy Spirit.
AMEN.

Father and sons
Lent script 4

This script, which may be appropriate for the fourth Sunday in Lent, needs the minimum movement and can be done anywhere. All it requires is three people of different ages with good natural voices rather than "stage" voices. To overplay the characters is to endanger what has sometimes been the very moving effect of the words.

They, more or less, are Jesus' words from Luke 15:11–32. All that has been done is to put them into the mouths of the people involved in the parable of the Prodigal Son and to let each character tell a separate part of the story.

The three characters can be located next to each other or around the room or hall, seated in chairs and standing only for their part of the story. A sung response, music or silence can be used to separate the parts.

Personnel: **A** *(the younger son, a late teenager)*
B *(the father, a man of 50 or over)*
C *(the elder son, in his twenties)*

A: My father had two sons.

One day, I, the younger, said to him,
"Father, give me my share of the property."
So my father divided the estate between the two
of us.

A few days later, I turned my share into cash
and left home with the money.

I went to a country far from home
where I wasted my money in reckless living.
I spent everything I had.

When I had nothing left,
a severe famine gripped the country
and I began to feel the pinch.

So I went to work for a local landowner,
who sent me out to his farm to take care of the
pigs.

I wished I could have filled myself
with the bean pods the pigs were eating,
but nobody gave me anything to eat.

Then, at last, I came to my senses.

I said to myself,
"All my father's hired laborers have more
than they can eat
and here I am about to starve.

I'll pack my bags and go back to my father
and tell him that I've sinned against God
and against him.

I'll tell him that I'm not fit to be called his son.
I'll ask him to treat me like one of his laborers."

So I got up and started back to my father.

B: He was still a long way off when I saw him
and my heart went out to him.
So I ran and threw my arms around him
and kissed him.

The boy said to me,
"Father, I have sinned against God and against you.
I am no longer fit to be called your son."

But I called my servants.

"Bring the best robe and put it on him," I said,
"Put a ring on his finger and shoes on his feet.

Get the prize calf and kill it
and let's celebrate with a feast.

For this son of mine was dead,
but now he's alive.
He was lost, but now he's found."

And then the fun began.

C: All this time, I was out in the field.

On my way back, as I came close to the house,
I heard music and dancing.

So I called one of the servants and asked him,
"What's all this about?"

"Your brother has come back home," he said,
"so your father has killed the prize calf
because he's got him back safe and sound."

I was so livid that I wouldn't go into the house.

Then my father came out and begged me to go in.

"Listen to me!" I said to him.
"You know that I've worked like a slave
for you for years;
and I've never disobeyed your orders.

But what have you ever given me?
Not even a goat I could kill
for a feast with my friends.

But this son of yours turns up
after wasting all your money on his women.
And what do you do?

You kill the prize calf for him!"

"Listen, son," my father said,
"You're always with me;
and everything I have is yours.
But we had to celebrate and be happy today.

Your brother here was dead,
but now he's alive.
He was lost, but now he's found."

You called your disciples

Lent prayer 6

Lord Jesus Christ,
you called your disciples to go forward with you
on the way to the cross.

Since you first walked that road
countless millions have followed you.

In all that we do as your disciples,
save us from false familiarity with your journey.
May we never presume to step into your shoes,
but make us small enough to fit our own,
and to walk in love and wonder behind you.
AMEN.

In days to come
Lent responses 5

This is a call to worship, adapted from Isaiah 2 & 11, and is particularly relevant to the fifth and sixth Sundays in Lent.

Leader: In days to come,
the mountain of the Lord's house
will be set over all other mountains,
raised high above all hills.

Nations will stream towards it
and many people will say,
ALL: LET US GO UP TO THE MOUNTAIN OF THE LORD,
TO THE HOUSE OF THE GOD OF JACOB,
THAT HE MAY TEACH US HIS WAYS,
AND THAT WE MAY WALK IN HIS PATHS.

Leader: Instruction comes from Jerusalem,
ALL: THE WORD OF THE LORD, FROM ZION.

He was going on a journey
Lent script 5

This script is best suited to the second Sunday before Easter.

It requires six readers, five of whom are placed around the circumference of the group or congregation. Only the person reading Jesus' part need be at the front or center.

The script is in five sections, each of which has a similar shape. The four voices, A, B, C and D, should follow each other in quick succession, the next beginning as the previous one says his or her last word. There should then be a short pause before the narrator speaks, and Jesus' words should be direct and calm, distinct from the first four voices, which are more agitated.

There is a longer pause after each section. The effect might be heightened by having a drumbeat or a repeated note on a glockenspiel played at these points.

The value of the script is also improved if it is neither introduced nor commented on. It is enough to precede and follow it with an appropriate hymn, song or incidental music; for example, it could be preceded by OH, WHERE ARE YOU GOING? (from the HEAVEN SHALL NOT WAIT collection) and followed by RIDE ON, RIDE ON, THE TIME IS RIGHT (from the ENEMY OF APATHY collection) or the more traditional RIDE ON, RIDE ON, IN MAJESTY.

Personnel: **A**
B
C
D
Narrator
Jesus

A: He was going on a journey ...

B: He was going on a journey ...

C: He was going on a journey ...

D: He was going on a journey ...

A: And Peter said,

B: And Thomas said,

C: And Andrew said,

D: And Judas said,

A: Where are you going?

B: Who is this man?

C: Which of us is greatest?

D: Lord, is it me?

Narrator: He was going on a journey
and Jesus said,

Jesus: Come with me.

(Pause)

A: He was going on a journey ...

B: He was going on a journey ...

C: He was going on a journey ...

D: He was going on a journey ...

A: And a young man said,

B: And a blind man said,

C: And a lunatic said,

D: And a leper said,

A: What must I do?

B: Take pity on me!

C: What do you want with us?

D: Lord, make me clean.

Narrator: He was going on a journey
and Jesus said,

Jesus: Do you want to get better?

(Pause)

A: He was going on a journey ...

B: He was going on a journey ...

C: He was going on a journey ...

D: He was going on a journey ...

A: And a woman in the crowd said,

B: And a woman at his side said,

C: And a woman at the well said,

D: And a woman on the road said,

A: Happy the womb that bore you!

B: Yes, it was me who touched you.

C: Can I have some of your water?

D: Lord, have mercy on me.

Narrator: He was going on a journey
and Jesus said,

Jesus: I will be with you always.

(Pause)

A: He was going on a journey ...

B: He was going on a journey ...

C: He was going on a journey ...

D: He was going on a journey ...

A: And John's disciples said,

B: And his home congregation said,

C: And the Pharisees said,

D: And the chief priests said,

A: Are you the one who is to come?

B: Could this be the carpenter's son?

C: Why does he eat with outcasts?

D: From where do you get your authority?

Narrator: He was going on a journey
and Jesus said,

Jesus: I have come that you might have life.

(Pause)

A: He was going on a journey ...

B: He was going on a journey ...

C: He was going on a journey ...

D: He was going on a journey ...

A: And the crowd were ready to say,

B: And the crowd were ready to cry,

C: And the crowd were ready to shout,

D: And the crowd were ready to scream,

A: Hosanna!

B: Blessings!

C: Barabbas!

D: Crucify him!

A, B, C & D: *(Shouting repeatedly and simultaneously and
                   getting gradually louder)*
                  HOSANNA!
                  BLESSINGS!
                  BARABBAS!
                  CRUCIFY HIM!

Narrator: Jesus was ahead of his disciples
                  who were filled with alarm;
                  the people who followed behind were afraid.

                  So Jesus took the twelve aside and said to them,

Jesus: We are going up to Jerusalem,
                  where the Son of Man will be handed over
                  to the chief priests and teachers of the Law.

                  They will condemn him to death
                  and then hand him over to the Gentiles,
                  who will mock him, spit on him and kill him;
                  but three days later,
                  he will rise to life.

                  Come, let us go forward.

He will walk
Lent meditation 4

Designed for two readers, this may also have a sung response between each section, such as BEHOLD THE LAMB OF GOD (from the COME ALL YOU PEOPLE collection).

At the front of the space, a rectangular table can be set up, facing away from the congregation. At the further end, there should be a cross and at the nearer an open Bible. Each time the response is sung a small votive candle is placed on the table, starting at the Bible and moving towards the cross. In this way, the direction of Jesus' journey is traced as the reading progresses.

Thereafter, a prayer about Jesus' and our journey might be said. The congregation could each have a small candle. The prayer may close with another sung response and people may be given the opportunity also to lay their candle along this line, as a sign of their intentions.

Personnel: **A**
B
Candle placer *(optional)*

A:

He will walk
a little in front of us
towards Jerusalem.

He will not be scared
though we are apprehensive.

If we try to discourage him,
he will recognize the Devil in our voice,
and he will tell us as much
in no uncertain terms.

Then he will go on again,
in faith,
towards Jerusalem.

(Sung response)

B: He will walk
a little in front of us
into controversy.

He will not be scared,
though we are apprehensive.

He will argue with the intelligent,
stop in their tracks the self-assured,
touch the diseased,
upset bank balances
by his outlandish behavior in the sanctuary,
and weep in public.

Then he will go on again,
in faith,
towards Jerusalem.

(Sung response)

A: He will walk
a little in front of us
into Gethsemane.

He will not be scared,
though we are apprehensive.

He will sweat blood
and ask God if there is another way.
And when God says no,
he will take the traitor's kiss,
the soldiers' spit
the bile and venom from the princes of religion.

Then he will go on again,
in faith,
towards the cross.

(Sung response)

B: He will walk
a little in front of us
towards Calvary.

He will not be scared,
no,
he will not be scared.

He will feel the pain
of wood and nails;
but more than this
he will feel the weight
of all the evil,
all the malice,
all the pettiness,
all the sin of the world
heaped upon his shoulders.

He will not throw off that weight,
though he could.

He will not give back evil for evil,
return malice for malice,
take revenge on the petty-minded,
or spew out hate
on all who have despised or rejected him.

He will not give back the sin of the world.
he will take it away ...
into death, into hell,
so that he can lead us into heaven.

Then he will go on again,
in faith,
towards the resurrection.

(Sung response)

A: He will walk
a little behind us
through the graveyard.

He will wait
until we realize that he has died
and admit our complicity in his life's ending.

Then he will come up behind us,
and say our name,
so that we can say his,
forever.

When the world could wait no longer

Lent litany 2

In its entirety, this litany of salvation includes elements from Isaiah's prophecy about the suffering servant, and ends with a post-resurrection credal statement. The first section may be used in Lent, with the entire text being most appropriate for Easter Day.

Leader: When the world could wait no longer,
Women: the carpenters took up their tools;
Men: God's son was made a cross,
Women: fashioned from wood and skill of human hands,
Men: fashioned from hate and will of human minds.

Leader: He was a man of sorrows and acquainted with grief;
ALL: FOR US HE GRIEVED.

Leader: He was summoned to the judgment hall;
an enemy of the state, a dange to religion.
ALL: FOR US HE WAS JUDGED.

Leader: He was lashed with tongues and scourged with thongs,
ALL: BY HIS WOUNDS, WE ARE HEALED.

Leader: He was nailed to the cross by human hands,
ALL: BONE OF OUR BONE, FLESH OF OUR FLESH.

(Easter Day section)

Leader: He died,
declaring God's forgiveness;
he rose again on the third day,
making it real;
he ascended into heaven,
that he might be everywhere on earth;
he sent the Holy Spirit,
as the seal of his intention.

Thus, though we were once no people,

ALL: NOW WE ARE GOD'S PEOPLE.

Leader: For God sent his Son into the world
not to condemn the world,

ALL: BUT THAT THE WORLD,
THROUGH HIM, MIGHT BE SAVED.

We have spoken about you

Lent prayer 7

A sung response such as HAVE MERCY ON US, LORD/ KHUDAYA RAHEM (from the LOVE & ANGER collection) or another KYRIE may be used between each part of the prayer. Suitable for Passion Sunday, the fifth Sunday in Lent, the words may also be appropriate for Maundy Thursday.

Leader: We have spoken about you
when it would have been better to stay silent;
and we have kept silent
when we should have said a word in your favor.

(Silence, followed by sung response)

Leader: We have preferred to think of our "cross"
as the sum total of our worries,
rather than the hard but essential task
which we alone can do for you.

(Silence, followed by sung response)

Leader: We have stayed with you
when people needed healing, teaching or telling off.
We enjoyed what you did for them and for us;
but there is a different tone in your voice now,
as if more is being asked of you
and you are asking more of us.
We are not sure how long we can stay with you.

(Silence, followed by sung response)

Leader: You are very patient with us,
even when you are annoyed with us.
Your smile is always kind, never nervous.
Knowing all, you still welcome us in your company
as if we had just arrived.

We will stay with you.

△ The cross
Lent responses 6

Leader: The cross,
ALL: WE WILL TAKE IT.

Leader: The bread,
ALL: WE WILL BREAK IT.

Leader: The pain,
ALL: WE WILL BEAR IT.

Leader: The joy,
ALL: WE WILL SHARE IT.

Leader: The Gospel,
ALL: WE WILL LIVE IT

Leader: The love,
ALL: WE WILL GIVE IT.

Leader: The light,
ALL: WE WILL CHERISH IT.

Leader: The darkness,
ALL: GOD SHALL PERISH IT.

↑ Palm Sunday
Lent symbolic action 1

Rather than import a donkey, other evocative symbols may be used on Palm Sunday:

a) Palm branches
... could either be the small and rather uncelebratory dried variety which are made into palm crosses, or people could collect excess foliage from trees and bushes, which they can wave more effectively.

b) Coats
... were strewn on Jesus' way. If the church has had a recent rummage or garage sale and a lot of rags are left, one possibility is to put these along the way of the procession (if there is one) or to strew them in the vestibule and down the aisles of the church. People will doubtless object, but the symbol has unquestionable biblical roots which the objectors may engage with for the first time.

c) Banners
... need not be the passive and predictable Palm Sunday variety, but may be more of the slogan type, either hand-held or hung on walls, evoking the kind of sentiments of that sector of the crowd who saw Christ as a politically combative savior, e.g.:

> *HOME RULE!*
> *STOP THE KILLINGS!*
> *CUT THE TAXES!*
> *SAY NO TO CAESAR!*
> *SOLDIERS GO HOME!*
> *FREE THE PEOPLE!*
> *FREE BARABBAS!*

I rejoiced

Lent responses 7

These opening responses, a paraphrase of Psalm 122, are particularly appropriate for the sixth Sunday in Lent, Passion or Palm Sunday.

Leader: I was glad when they said to me,
     "Let us go to the house of the Lord."
ALL: AND LOOK, NOW WE STAND IN THAT PLACE,
     IN THE CITY BELOVED OF GOD.

Leader: Jerusalem proudly is built,
     to gather the people together.
ALL: SHE WELCOMES THE CHILDREN OF GOD
     WHO WORSHIP THEIR MAKER IN UNITY.

Leader: Here they give thanks to the Lord
     according to God's deep desire;
ALL: HERE IS OUR MONARCH'S OWN COURT
     AND THE THRONES OF THE HOUSEHOLD OF FAITH.

Leader: Pray for the peace of Jerusalem:
     may they prosper whose love is for you.
ALL: PEACE BE WITHIN YOUR WALLS
     AND PROSPERITY BE IN YOUR PALACES.

Leader: For the sake of my family and friends,
     I will say, "May God's peace be in you."
ALL: OUT OF LOVE FOR THE HOUSE OF THE LORD,
     I WILL PRAY FOR ITS WELL-BEING FOREVER.

Rejoice, rejoice
Lent responses 8

These responses are adapted from Zechariah 9 and are particularly appropriate for Palm Sunday.

Leader: Rejoice, rejoice, you sons of Zion!
Shout for joy, you daughters of Jerusalem!
Look and see,
your king is coming to you.

ALL: HE COMES TRIUMPHANT AND VICTORIOUS,
YET HUMBLE AND RIDING ON A DONKEY.

Leader: The Lord now will save his people
as a shepherd saves his flock from danger.

ALL: LIKE PRECIOUS STONES IN A CROWN,
WE WILL SHINE IN GOD'S OWN LAND.

I It was on the Sunday (i)
Lent reading 2

This reading was originally printed as part of a larger piece consisting of the other IT WAS ON ... readings found in this book. It was primarily intended to be read by people on their own, as personal preparation for a series of workshops and reflections during Holy Week.

It was on the Sunday
that he took on the city.

Religious freaks usually appear in the desert
urging people to come into the open air
and find God through getting back to nature.
God, you see, doesn't live in the city.
He prefers the smell of a garden to that of a gutter.
He likes to see children playing beside streams,
not hanging out on the sidewalk.
And far better in his eyes are lovers lounging in the long grass
than shacking up in a single bed.

The city is for sin.
God doesn't go there.

The Lord is my Shepherd,
not my social worker.
He makes me to lie down in green pastures,
not shrinks' couches.
He leads me beside still waters,
not trickles of urine from a beggar's bladder.
And on the mountains are the peace messenger's feet beautiful,
not in the middle of the road.

It was on the Sunday
that he took on the city.

Humble and riding on a donkey
Lent responses 9

Leader: Humble and riding on a donkey,
ALL: WE GREET YOU.

Leader: Acclaimed by crowds and caroled by children,
ALL: WE CHEER YOU.

Leader: Moving from the peace of the countryside
to the corridors of power,
ALL: WE SALUTE YOU, CHRIST OUR LORD.

Leader: You are giving the beasts of burden
a new dignity;
you are giving majesty
a new face;
you are giving those who long for redemption
a new song to sing.
ALL: WITH THEM, WITH HEART AND VOICE,
WE SHOUT "HOSANNA!"

Ride on, ride on
Lent prayer 8

Like the last set of responses, this participative prayer may be used on Palm Sunday.

Leader: Lord Jesus Christ,
... over the broken glass of our world,
the rumors meant to hurt,
the prejudice meant to wound,
the weapons meant to kill,
ride on ...
trampling our attempts at disaster into dust.
ride on,

ALL: RIDE ON IN MAJESTY

Leader: ... over the distance
which separates us from you,
and it is such a distance,
measurable in half truths,
        in unkept promises,
        in second-best obedience,
ride on ...
until you touch and heal us,
who feel for no one but ourselves.
ride on,

ALL: RIDE ON IN MAJESTY

Leader: ... through the back streets
and the sin bins
and the sniggered-at corners of the city,
where human life festers
and love runs cold,
ride on ...
bringing hope and dignity
where most send scorn and silence.
ride on,

ALL: RIDE ON IN MAJESTY.

Leader: For you, O Christ, do care
and must show us how.
On our own,
our ambitions rival your summons
and thus threaten good faith
and neglect God's people.

In your company and at your side,
we might yet help to bandage and heal
the wounds of the world.
ride on,

ALL: RIDE ON IN MAJESTY
AND TAKE US WITH YOU.
AMEN.

Holy Week
resources

Jesus, Prince of Peace

Holy Week litany 1

If desired a sung response, a KYRIE or similar may be inserted between each section.

Personnel: **A**
B
C

A: Jesus,
Prince of Peace,
humble and riding on a donkey.

B: Jesus,
disturber of the peace,
you upset bad religion
when it gets in the way of God.

C: Jesus,
upsetter of the self-righteous,
you turn questions on their head,
offering no instant answers,
but showing the way.

D: Jesus,
lover of the lost,
you say "forgive"
when we want to shout "condemn!"

E: Jesus,
host at the table,
you share your best
even in the face of our worst.

F: Jesus,
Savior of the world
... yes, even the world
which wants you
until it meets you.

In the Temple
Holy Week symbolic action 1

The Monday of Holy Week is the day when Jesus overturned the money stalls in the Temple, called it a house of prayer for all nations, healed the sick and praised the children who sang to him.

All of these aspects of the day's events suggest the possible use of a range of objects or symbols, for example, coins, flags, medicine bottles, teddy bears. If objects are not used, posters instead may depict images. These might be photographic (e.g., of children) or drawn (e.g., the symbol of a snake on a branch, a biblical symbol from the story of Moses when he raised the serpent on a stick and all who looked on it were healed).

Four places, or stations, in the worship space may be devoted to these symbols. The object or poster may be placed there after the reading of each of the relevant parts of the story in Matthew 21:12–17.

Thereafter, prayers may be said for each of the groups of people evoked by the symbols. During a sung response or chant, the congregation may be invited to leave their seats and light a candle at the appropriate station for those they want to pray for.

A house of prayer for all nations
Holy Week script 1

A script which deals with the widely differing ways we can see God's house, be it a repository of tradition or a place of happy memories, and how this measures up to Jesus' understanding of it.

Towards the end, a table with a bowl of coins on it should be overturned. It may be more effective if this is located behind the congregation.

Note: The date 1662 (Anglican Prayer Book) should be substituted by another appropriate historic date, according to denomination.

The prayer IF WE HAVE USED YOUR HOUSE (page 88) may follow the script.

Personnel:	***Narrator***
	A
	B
	C

Narrator: My house ...

A: My grandfather helped to build it.

B: My father sat here.

C: That's the family pew.

A: He loved his church, he did.

B: Sat here until the day he died.

C: It's got nice embroidered kneelers.

Narrator: My house shall be called ...

A: A neo-gothic masterpiece.

B:	A beautiful memorial window.
C:	Somewhere to get your batteries charged.
Narrator:	My house shall be called a house of prayer.
A:	They don't appreciate it, the young ones.
B:	I mean, if 1662 was good enough for God, it's ...
C:	... all about tradition, we need tradition.
A:	Nobody likes these new hymns ...
B:	or sharing the peace ...
C:	or these women priests.
Narrator:	My house shall be called a house of prayer.
A:	Matins once a month.
B:	Baptisms, weddings and funerals.
C:	Christmas and Easter, I wouldn't miss them.
A:	I don't think you need to understand.
B:	I always give lilies on the Sunday nearest my mother's death.
C:	It's good for the children.
Narrator:	My house shall be called a house of prayer for ...
A:	for the President;
B:	for all Americans;
C:	for emergencies.
Narrator:	My house shall be called a house of prayer for all nations.
A:	Not the people in the scheme, they wouldn't darken the door.

B: Not the charismatics,
they like that happy-clappy kind of thing.

C: Not the foreigners,
not with their strange customs and smells.

Narrator: ... for all nations.

A: I mean, they wouldn't understand.

B: they wouldn't feel at home.

C: they'd want to dance or something.

Narrator: My house shall be called a house of prayer for all
nations.

A: I know they're the same, but they're different.

B: Marxists ... that's what these ecumaniacs are.

C: So what if the church commissioners have
money in arms companies?

A: We need the money for the bell tower,

B: the organ fund,

C: the roof.

Narrator: Jesus went into the Temple
and drove out all those who were buying and selling
there.

He overturned the tables of the moneychangers

(Table and coins are overturned)

and the stools of those who sold pigeons
and said to them:

"It is written in Scripture that God said,
'My temple will be called a house of prayer for all
nations.' But you are making it a hideout for
thieves."

It was on the Monday
Holy Week reading 1

This reading was originally printed as part of a larger piece consisting of the other IT WAS ON ... readings found in this book. It was primarily intended to be read by people on their own, as personal preparation for a series of workshops and reflections during Holy Week.

Alternatively, it may be read in a similar way, but on its own on the Monday of Holy Week.

It was on the Monday
that religion got in the way.

An outsider would have thought
that it was a pet shop's fire sale.
And the outsider, in some ways,
wouldn't have been far wrong.

Only, it wasn't household pets,
it was pigeons that were being purchased.
And it wasn't a fire sale;
it was a rip-off stall in a holy temple
bartering birds for sacrifice.
And the price was something only the rich could
afford.
No discounts to students, pensioners,
or social security claimants.

Then he,
the holiest man on earth,
went through the bizarre bazaar
like a bull in a china shop.
So the doves got liberated
and the pigeon sellers got angry.
And the police went crazy
and the poor people clapped like mad,
because he was making a sign
that God was for everybody,
not just for those who could afford him.
He turned the tables on Monday ...
The day that religion got in the way.

⃝ He healed them
Holy Week intercessions 1

During these prayers for the Monday of Holy Week, people can be invited to make a request of God in silence. At the end of each section, a sung response, such as LORD JESUS CHRIST, LOVER OF ALL (from the HEAVEN SHALL NOT WAIT collection) or O LORD, HEAR MY PRAYER from Taizé, may be used.

Leader: On the Monday of Holy week,
                 the crippled and the blind came to Jesus in the
Temple
                 and he healed them.
                 So let us pray for
                 those who are crippled by disease or anxiety;

                 (Silence, then sung response)

                 ... those who are crippled by a system;

                 (Silence, then sung response)

                 ... those who are blind to beauty, love and peace;

                 (Silence, then sung response)

                 ... those who are blind to what they must do now or do
                 next;

                 (Silence, then sung response)

                 ... the church in places where it has the possibility
                 of healing the wounds of the nations;

                 (Silence, then sung response)

                 ... and for ourselves we pray,
                 that we may discern a clear vision of your kingdom;
                 and that we may steadily walk your path,
                 Jesus Christ, our Lord.
                 AMEN.

If we have used your house
Holy Week prayer 1

This may be used after the script A HOUSE OF PRAYER FOR ALL NATIONS on page 83.

Leader: If we have used your house for our purposes
as if you did not mind or it did not matter,
ALL: LORD, FORGIVE US.

Leader: If we have cosseted your house in tradition,
rather than hallowed it by prayer,
ALL: LORD, FORGIVE US.

Leader: If we have made it a house for one nation,
or part of a nation,
or for part of the Church,
ALL: LORD, FORGIVE US.

Leader: And if we can see clearly
the misuse others make of your house
and are blind to our own malpractices,
ALL: LORD, FORGIVE US.

Leader: Kindle in us and in all your people
the desire to make all your sanctuaries
the shop windows of heaven
rather than religious theme parks of earth.

We ask this for your own name's sake.
AMEN.

It was on the Tuesday
Holy Week reading 2

This reading was originally printed as part of a larger piece consisting of the other IT WAS ON ... readings found in this book. It was primarily intended to be read by people on their own, as personal preparation for a series of workshops and reflections during Holy Week.

Alternatively, it may be read in a similar way, but on its own on the Tuesday of Holy Week.

It was on the Tuesday
that he let them have it.

If you had been there
you would have thought
that a union official was being taken to task
by a group of mobsters.
Or that the chairman of a multinational corporation
was being interrogated by left-wing activists
posing as shareholders.

They wanted to know why
and they wanted to know how.

They were the respectable men,
the influential men,
the establishment.

The questions they asked
ranged from silly schoolgirl speculations
about whether you would be a bigamist in heaven
if you had married twice on earth,
to what was the central rule of civilized behavior.

They knew the answers already ...
or so they thought,
otherwise they would never have asked the
questions.

And like most of us
they were looking for an argument
with no intention of a change of heart.

So he flailed them with his tongue ...
those who tried to look interested
but never wanted to be committed.

And that was on the Tuesday ...
the day when he let them ...
let us ...
have it.

The tree
Holy Week meditation 1

The story of Jesus cursing the fruit tree is one of the more obscure in the Gospels, until we realize that God expects fruit from all believers in and out of season.

When this meditation was first used, people had been asked to draw a tree and talk to each other about what they had drawn and why. The drawings were then gathered in and, during Jesus' words of cursing, as people had their eyes shut, there was a sound of paper being torn, which the participants took to be their fondly drawn trees. In fact, scrap paper was employed, but the feeling that something that belonged to them was being destroyed added to the poignancy of the meditation.

If using the meditation in worship, making drawings would probably prove impractical. However, if it is done there should be a time of corporate reflection after the meditation, which is not necessary if it is simply read as written.

The reading should be followed by music, or a sung response, such as a KYRIE ELEISON, may be used and people should be encouraged to close their eyes and use their imaginations to picture the happenings. The two readers should be located in different parts of the worship area.

Personnel: **Narrator**
             Jesus

Narrator: Imagine yourself as a tree ...
              standing at a crossroads
              where two country lanes meet;
              standing up a bit, back from the road,
              with a view of the surrounding countryside;
              standing in the warmest of days ...
              warm, but not scorching,
              warm enough
              to make you feel at one with the world,

and glad to be where you are.

Feel for your roots ...
      buried deep below you,
      toes which you can't wiggle,
      but which you know are there ...
      deep, deep in the warm, moist earth.

Feel for your bark ...
      showing the signs of age,
      but not cruelly;
      a bark which can tell stories
      like an old woman's weather-beaten face.

Feel for your branches ...
      stretching out like arms and fingers,
      resting places for the birds,
      sheltering places for travelers caught in a
         storm.

Feel for your leaves ...
      fluttering in the gentle breeze,
      fully grown, green and full of life.

You are a happy tree ...
      proud to be where you are,
      glad to be the way you are.

So being at one with yourself,
you look across the countryside in front of you ...
you look towards fields of sheep,
fields of cattle,
fields where corn is turning from green to yellow,
fields where the earth is damp brown
because just today potatoes were harvested,
and you can see sacks stacked together
every fifty yards.

As you look around
you see people coming up the road
on your right-hand side ...
about forty-five degrees to your right ...
the little narrow road
only ever used by tractors
and children going for a picnic down by the
   lakeside.

Up this road towards you
is coming a group of young men ...
about ten of them.

At first you wonder whether they are the kind
who might break off a branch just for devilment,
or carve their initials on your bark,
or climb up and sit heavily on you.

But they do not look that type.
They are smiling ... tired smiles ...
as if they have walked a distance and are weary.

They come closer towards you.
You don't recognize them.
They are not local boys ...
you know that because they are looking at you.
Local people just walk by.
They are coming closer and looking at you
and one of them –
a man who looks in his late twenties
with jet black hair and a newly trimmed beard –
walks through the group towards you.

You hear him speak.

Jesus: Yes ... it's a lovely tree.

Narrator: You appreciate him admiring you.

Jesus: Yes, it's a lovely tree.

Narrator: His eyes are now looking at your branches ...

Jesus: But I'm not looking for beauty.
I'm hungry ... I'm looking for food.

Narrator: And you think ...
well, he'll not find any.
It's too early.
I've just got leaves.
I've got the beginnings of flowers on some
    branches.
Another week and they'll be out.
But no fruit ...

Jesus: I'm hungry, I'm looking for food.

Narrator: But doesn't he know that it's the wrong season?
Stupid man.
Stupid man.

Jesus: Curse you!
Curse you!
From now on ...
from now on, no one ...
no one will ever eat fruit from you again.

(Pause)

Narrator: And you feel ... in your leaves,
in your branches,
in your roots,
in yourself ...
How do you feel?

(Pause)

The man turns his back on you.
His friends look at him in astonishment.
They are silent.
It seems they don't know what to say.
They look at you, almost in sympathy ...
and they walk away,
along the road to your left.

One or two of them
occasionally turn their heads and look back ...
but not the man with the jet black hair
and the newly trimmed beard.
He doesn't look back ...

He's got other things on his mind ...

He is hungry.

↑ Anointing
Holy Week symbolic action 2

In the Old Testament, anointing commonly signified a transmission of power and blessing. In the New Testament, it came to be a sign of love, of identity as a Christian and of the reception of the gifts of the Holy Spirit. These flowed from the Church's understanding of Jesus as the "Messiah" or "Christ," which means "the anointed one."

At Iona Abbey, the service on the Wednesday of Holy Week often includes an act of anointing, recalling the occasion in Simon the Leper's house when the woman anointed Jesus as an act of love which he interpreted as a preparation for his burial.

The act of anointing usually happens in the middle or towards the end of the service. During instrumental music or an appropriate chant, such as TAKE O TAKE ME AS I AM (from the COME ALL YOU PEOPLE collection), the congregation may, if they wish, leave their seats and go to one of three or four different locations in the church. In the Abbey, the communion table, the font and the South Aisle are used, not so much for any special significance, but for the fact that they are not in full view of all. Being at the edge of the worship space, they are thus appropriate for what is a quiet and fairly intimate symbolic action.

In each of these locations there is a person, preferably a woman (in echo of the Gospel story), who stands holding a small bowl of perfumed oil. She draws the sign of the cross on the palm of each person and they return to their seats. Once all those who wish to receive anointing have done so, the women themselves return to their seats and a blessing is said.

△ We will remember the soothing
Holy Week responses 1

Leader: We will remember the soothing,
ALL: AND NOT FORGET THE JARRING.

Leader: We will remember the sweetness,
ALL: AND NOT FORGET THE SOUR.

Leader: We will remember the jagged desperateness of
Judas,
ALL: AND OWN IT;
IT IS OUR STORY TOO.

Leader: We will remember
Women: the passion of love,
Men: the smell of perfume,
Women: the pain of rejection,
Men: the stench of blood money.

Leader: And to help us on the journey,
to help us hold the tensions,
to help us face both the delight and the difficulty,
ALL: WE WILL SAY YES
TO GOD'S GENEROSITY IN CREATION,
WE WILL SAY YES
TO GOD'S JUDGMENT POURED OUT ON
HUMANKIND,
WE WILL SAY YES
TO GOD'S JUSTICE IN JESUS.

It was on the Wednesday
Holy Week reading 3

This reading was originally printed as part of a larger piece consisting of the other IT WAS ON ... readings found in this book. It was primarily intended to be read by people on their own, as personal preparation for a series of workshops and reflections during Holy Week.

Alternatively, it may be read in a similar way, but on its own on the Wednesday of Holy Week.

It was on the Wednesday
that they called him a wasteful person.

The place smelled like the perfume department
of a big store.

It was as if somebody had bumped an elbow
against a bottle
and sent it crashing to the floor,
setting off the most expensive stink bomb on earth.

But it happened in a house,
not a shop.

And the woman who broke the bottle
was no casual afternoon shopper.
She was the poorest of the poor,
giving away the only precious thing she had.

And he sat still
while she poured the liquid all over his head ...
as unnecessary as aftershave
on a full crop of hair and a bearded chin.

And those who smelled it,
and those who saw it,
and those who remembered
that he was against extravagance,

called him a wasteful person.
They forgot
that he also was the poorest of the poor.

And they who had much
and who had given him nothing,
objected to a pauper giving him everything.

Jealousy was in the air
when a poor woman's generosity
became an embarrassment to their tight-fistedness ...

That was on the Wednesday,
when they called him a wasteful person.

I will give what I have

Holy Week reading 4

It was on the Wednesday of Holy Week that the story of the woman who anointed Jesus occurred. It is she who is represented in these words. The music to which they can be sung can be found in the ENEMY OF APATHY collection, but they can be read on their own equally effectively.

From a high, secret shelf, I take what I hid myself –
perfume, precious and rare, never meant to spill or spare.
This I'll carefully break, this I'll empty for his sake:
I will give what I have to my Lord.

Though the action is crude, it will show my gratitude
for the truth that I've learned from the one who's
    heaven-sent;
for this life once a mess which his beauty can express,
I will give what I have to my Lord.

With his critics around, common gossip will abound.
They'll note all that they see to discredit him and me.
Let them smirk, let them jeer, say what people want to
    hear;
I will give what I have to my Lord.

It's because he'll receive, that I believe
God has time for the poor. He has shown us heaven's door.
Be it perfume and care, be it anger or despair,
I will give what I have to my Lord.

↑ Maundy Thursday (i)
Holy Week symbolic action 3

At Iona Abbey, the Maundy Thursday liturgy has three venues. This model may be transferable or adaptable elsewhere.

a) The Lord's Supper
The sacrament takes place not in the church but in an upstairs room or hall. Instead of an altar, tables are often assembled in a goal-post formation and covered with a white cloth and candles. Everyone sits around the celebrant in the middle.

If the foot-washing ceremony is to happen, it can take place in the middle of the assembly rather than on altar stairs and the foot washer(s) may go among the congregation rather than have members come forward.

If the church's regular practice is to use individual communion glasses and diced bread, this may be an appropriate time to change and use common cups or chalices and pita breads or an unsliced loaf.

If the normal practice is to have people come forward and stand in front of the altar, the more historically authentic practice of sending around the bread and cups (with purificators or napkins) might be more evocative.

People simply need to know what is going to happen in advance. It should be indicated or stated that communion will be shared in a more random fashion than usual, and people should have no difficulty in indicating to stewards or to each other where the bread and wine need to be passed. A quiet chant sung during the receiving of communion helps take the edge off the atmosphere. THIS IS THE BODY OF CHRIST from the THERE IS ONE AMONG US collection would be one such possibility.

After the bread and wine have come back to the table, there is a brief prayer, but no dismissal. Instead the congregation begin to sing a recessional which takes them to the next venue. Psalm 23 to the tune CRIMOND, sung until all have reached the next space, is very appropriate, especially since many people will know the words by heart.

b) The garden
In Iona Abbey, people move into and around the cloisters, which is an open-air venue. In other places, people may move into the church garden. Torches or weather-safe candles may be used.

Here, when all are assembled, there is silence and either that portion of scripture alluding to the betrayal in the garden may be read, followed by a silence, or SIT HERE WHILE I PRAY on page 118.

After the reading, people should move quickly, but in silence, to the next venue.

c) The church
This should be fully lit and people encouraged to stand around at the back, looking towards the chancel.

What is commonly known as "the stripping of the altar" now takes place. STRIPPING THE CHURCH (page 120) gives more detail. What happens essentially is that Psalm 22 is read antiphonally and a team of people rush through the congregation towards the front and begin to remove all ornamentation from the sanctuary.

That means plants, crosses, pictures, ornaments, altar cloths, pulpit bibles, etc. These should be taken to a designated area or room, the whole thing done with a sense of coldness or urgency.

As the ornamentation is removed, so the lights in the church gradually dim, until only a small proportion of the congregation is able to see the text. When the Psalm is finished, people leave quickly and in silence, in order to sense the abandonment which Christ felt.

As with the Communion, people should be warned in advance that there will be no dismissal, but some people should be primed to leave the church immediately so that the rest will follow.

From now until the end of the Easter Vigil, it is appropriate to have no instrumental music, only unaccompanied singing.

Maundy Thursday (ii)
Holy Week script 2

As its title suggests, this script deals with the incidents leading up to the evening before the crucifixion. It is a review of some of the main events of Holy Week and is frequently used as a prelude to the sacrament of Holy Communion.

At its first performance in the English Reformed Church in Amsterdam, the chancel area looked in disarray with upturned tables and chairs. It was from this location that the stallholder spoke and, at the end of the script, during a hymn, the characters rearranged the furniture and laid tables, enabling the sacrament to flow from the action.

Not all the speaking, however, should be done from the front.

The narrator and Jesus should be at the back of the congregation, Jesus being unseen until, at the end, he walks forward to wash Peter's feet.

The cynic may speak from an upstairs gallery, a good place in which to be an onlooker, or from a side aisle. The stallholder, if not speaking from the disordered chancel, may stand beside an upturned table in another side aisle or against a wall.

Towards the front left should be four chairs facing away from the congregation on which the Pharisees can sit throughout or during an interlude before their speaking part begins. Towards the front right should be another four chairs on which the four disciples can sit. Of these four, two may be Peter and Judas. At the point at which it is alluded that the disciples went to the house of Simon the Leper, the chairs should be turned inwards in order that Jesus may be seen to wash Peter's feet.

No particular dress is required for the script, though it is helpful to have the four Pharisees identified with each other by similar costume or a common accessory, e.g., the same scarf or tie.

It's not advisable to try to do the script in "period costume" as this inevitably makes it look like something which took over where the church nativity play left off. It also gives the impression that the events of Holy Week are for yesterday and not today.

It is however advised that music be used to link the various scenes. It may be sufficient to have THE PASSION CHORALE (O SACRED HEAD SORE WOUNDED) played between each section. But that can only happen if the organist can play sensitively and the organ does not make heavy respiratory sounds when not being played which prevent the dialogue from being heard.

An alternative might be to get someone to play that or another tune on the recorder. Or the choir or, better still, the congregation might sing an appropriate response between the scenes. Examples would be either a KYRIE (from the Russian Orthodox tradition or the Taizé Community) or WONDER AND STARE (from the COME ALL YOU PEOPLE collection).

Personnel: **Cynic**
                 Narrator
                 Jesus
                 Stallholder
                 Pharisee A
                 Pharisee B
                 Pharisee C
                 Pharisee D
                 Disciple A
                 Disciple B/Peter
                 Disciple C
                 Disciple D/Judas

Cynic: I cannot say I was very impressed, were you?

                 Or perhaps you didn't see it –
                 the royal procession, I mean.
                 We're used to processions in this city,
                 and demonstrations.
                 All it needs is for some foreign princess
                 or secretary of state to come for afternoon tea
                 and the crowds gather ...
                 lining the route, blocking the streets, waving madly
                 and all desperate to get a wave back.

                 But this thing, this today,
                 was worse, much worse.
                 It was all rather disgusting and ... cheap?
                 Yes ... cheap!

Why the crowds went wild,
I don't quite understand,
nor do I want to.

Oh yes, I caught a glimpse.
I do live above the main street after all ...
I could hardly help hearing the racket.
I looked out ...
and there it ... he ... was

A young man on a young horse on a hot day.

Poor fool.

I don't know who put him up to it,
but whoever was responsible
must have a very perverted sense of humor.

Our city has enough fools in it
without adding to their number
or giving them a king.

Everybody, of course, is talking about it ...
the people here have such a taste for scandal.
I just hope that by now
someone has rescued the poor devil
before he's put up to something more serious.

(Music)

Narrator: Jesus went up to the Temple
and there he found the dealers in cattle, sheep and
    pigeons,
and the moneylenders at the tables.
He made a whip out of cords
and drove them out of the Temple,
sheep, cattle and all.
He upset the tables of the moneychangers,
scattering their coins.
Then he turned on the dealers of pigeons.

Jesus: Out!
Take them out!
You must not turn my Father's house into a market.
It is to be a house of prayer for all nations.
But you have made it a robber's cave!

Stallholder: *(Leaning on an upturned table)*
Twenty years I've had a stall here
and my father worked in the Temple before me.
We've had some weird types in our time
and we've had arguments ...
oh yes, we've had arguments.
But never an outrage like we had today.

In comes this stranger with his friends
and a whole crowd of children,
and the next thing we know
he's running about shouting
and knocking everything everywhere.
I mean, aside from anything else,
someone could have gotten hurt ...
and what an example to show the children.

You see this table ...
it's my table.
Half an hour ago it was covered
with what I had to sell.
Pigeons for ...
God, I suppose ...
but I don't ask questions;
I'm just here to make money.

The trouble with him of course,
is that he doesn't respect tradition.
Yes ... he doesn't respect tradition.
We have a way of working in this place.
We've got a religion that's been going on
much longer than this building
and it's what people like.
It's what they're used to.
You can't just burst into a church
and tell them that they've got it all wrong.

I mean, religion is all about tradition, isn't it?
Religion's not meant to change.
People need something in their lives
which is always there.
That's why this building is here.
That's why I'm selling things to keep the people happy.

Why the police didn't come and arrest him,
I'll never know.
Some say they were afraid of public opinion,

afraid there would be a riot.
You see, he's well in with the crowd.

Now if he were a respectable, well-educated man ...
I might have listened to him.
But these upstarts from the working class
with their funny accents ...
they don't know their place.
Give them a bit of support and ...
and they think they're God.

(Music during which the Pharisees may move to their seats)

Narrator: Jesus left the Temple and spent the night in
            Bethany.
         He returned to Jerusalem next morning
         and entered the Temple.
         There the chief priests and elders of the nation
         came to him with questions.
         At the same time,
         Pharisees and lawyers devised a plan
         by which they intended to trap him with his own
            words
         and they sent a delegation to join the questioning.

(The Pharisees stand up one by one as they speak, directing their words to Jesus at the back of the building)

Pharisee A: Jesus, by what authority
             are you acting the way you do?
             Who gave you that authority?

Pharisee B: Jesus, haven't you said
             that we can't serve two masters?
             Then is it right to pay taxes to Caesar?

Pharisee C: Jesus, isn't it true
             that you believe in the resurrection of the dead?
             Then can there be marriage in heaven?

Pharisee D: Jesus, don't you claim to fulfill all the law?
             Then which is the greatest of the law's
                commandments?

Pharisee A: Jesus, who gave you authority?

Pharisee B: Jesus, is it right to pay taxes?

Pharisee C: Jesus, is there marriage in heaven?

Pharisee D: Jesus, which law is the greatest?

Pharisee A: Who gave you authority?

Pharisee B: Is it right to pay taxes?

Pharisee C: Is there marriage in heaven?

Pharisee D: Which law is the greatest?

Jesus: *(Shouting)*

Alas!
Alas for you, lawyers and Pharisees ... hypocrites!
You shut the door of the kingdom of heaven
in people's faces.
You do not enter yourselves
and when others are entering you stop them.

Alas, alas for you, lawyers and Pharisees.
You travel over land and sea to make one convert
and when you have won him,
you make him twice as fit for hell
as you are yourselves.

Alas, alas for you.
You are like tombs covered with whitewash.
They look well from the outside,
but inside they are covered with corpses' bones.

O Jerusalem, Jerusalem ...
the city that murders the prophets
and stones the messengers sent to her!
How often I would have gathered your children
as a hen gathers her chickens under her wings ...
but you would not let me.

(Music during which the Pharisees resume their seats)

Narrator: Jesus told them a story ...
when the Son of Man comes in all his glory
and all the angels with him,

he shall separate the people of the nations into two
    groups,
as a shepherd separates the sheep from the goats,
and he will place the sheep on his right hand
and the goats on his left.
Then the king will say to those on his right hand:

Jesus: You have my Father's blessing;
come, enter and possess the kingdom
that has been made ready for you
since the world was made.

For when I was hungry, you gave me food;
when thirsty, you gave me drink;
when I was a stranger you took me into your home;
when naked, you clothed me;
when I was ill you came to my help;
when in prison, you visited me.

Narrator: Then the righteous will reply:

(The Disciples stand and turn as they speak)

Disciple A: Lord, when was it we saw you hungry and fed you?

Disciple B: Lord, when was it we saw you thirsty and gave you a
drink?

Disciple C: Lord, when was it we saw you a stranger and took
you in?

Disciple D: Lord, when was it we saw you naked and clothed
you?

Disciples: LORD, WHEN DID WE SEE YOU ILL OR IN PRISON
AND CAME TO VISIT YOU?

Narrator: And the king will reply:

Jesus: I tell you this:
anything you did for one of my brothers or sisters
    here,
however humble,
you did for me.

Narrator: Then he will say to those on his left hand:

Jesus:	The curse is upon you; go from my sight to the eternal fire that is ready for the Devil and his angels. For when I was hungry, you gave me nothing to eat; when thirsty, nothing to drink; when I was a stranger, you gave me no home; when naked, you did not clothe me; when I was ill or in prison, you did not come to my help.
Narrator:	And they too will reply:
Pharisee A:	Lord, when was it that we saw you hungry?
Pharisee B:	Lord, when was it that we saw you thirsty?
Pharisee C:	Lord, when was it that we saw you a stranger?
Pharisee D:	Lord, when was it that we saw you naked?
Pharisees:	AND WHEN DID WE SEE YOU ILL OR IN PRISON?
Jesus:	I tell you this ... *(Pharisees turn their backs)* anything you did not do for one of these, however humble, you did not do for me.
Narrator:	And they will go away to eternal punishment, and the righteous will enter eternal life. *(Music during which the Pharisees confer together in a corner and the disciples rearrange the chairs to face inwards)* Then the chief priests and the elders of the nation met in the place of the high priests; and there they conferred together on a scheme to have Jesus arrested by some trick and put to death. *(Pharisees mumble to each other before speaking aloud)*
Pharisee A:	It must not be during the festival.

Pharisees: WHY NOT?

Pharisee A: There may be rioting among the people.

                (They remain standing in a huddle)

Narrator: Jesus was at Bethany
in the house of Simon the Leper,
when a woman came to him
with a small bottle of fragrant oil which was very
    costly;
and as he sat at the table,
she began to pour it over his head.
The disciples – or at least one of them –
objected ...

*(Judas withdraws from the disciples and stands
aside, moving eventually towards the Pharisees)*

Then Judas Iscariot, one of the twelve,
went to the chief priests to betray Jesus.
When they heard what he had come for,
they were greatly pleased.

Judas: How much will you give me to betray him?

*(The Pharisees turn towards Judas and one of them
clinks thirty pieces of silver into a purse during
Judas' speech. All the officials look dour, directing
their gaze at him. Judas speaks to the congregation,
to himself, or to the Pharisees as the words suggest)*

There ...
I've said it, I've said it,
I've said it.
And now ... I feel much better.
It's a weight off my shoulders,
it's a burden off my mind,
it's a great relief ...

(Pause)

... is it hell!
It's hell ...
and it's still hell ...
and ...
well,
somebody had to do it.

Somebody had to handle the dirty goods.
He has to die –
he said it himself,
I'm only helping him on his way ...
on to a cross.

But who knows,
maybe he needs this.
Maybe this will rouse him
to display all the power he's supposed to have.

Maybe I'm doing him a good turn.
Maybe he'll even say, "Thank you, Judas."

Oh Judas!

(Pause)

Well, they know I'm a thief anyway.
They know my reputation and so does he.
I may as well live up to my name.
After all,
I don't claim to be the "savior of the world,"
I just claim to be myself.
Anyone in my situation would do exactly the same
    thing.
Wouldn't you ...
... if the money was good enough?
... if you couldn't live with your jealousy?
... if you didn't know whether you were loved?

(To the Pharisees)

How much did you say?

(Snatches money and looks at it)

Is that all?
Is that all he's worth?
Is that all the hell in my head is worth?

Thirty pieces of silver ...
just enough to buy a piece of rope to hang myself
and a burial plot for my body.

I'm only joking, of course.

Of course, I'm only joking.

(Starts to offer money back to the Pharisees)

Of course, I'm only joking.

(Beseeching them to take the money back, but Pharisees point to the door)

Of course...

Narrator: On the first day of unleavened bread,
when the Passover lambs were being slaughtered,
his disciples said to him:

Disciple B: *(Stands)*

Where would you like us to go
and prepare for the Passover supper?

Narrator: So he sent two of his disciples with these
instructions:

Jesus: Go into the city and tell a certain man,
"The Master says,
'My appointed time is near;
I am to keep the Passover with my disciples at your
house.' "

Narrator: The disciples did as Jesus directed.
They prepared for the Passover
and in the evening he came to the house with the
twelve.

*(Music during which Disciples A and B go outside.
They may return with bread and wine if
appropriate.)*

Jesus knew that his hour had come,
that he must leave the world and go to the Father.
He had always loved his own who were in the
world,
and now he was to show the full extent of his love.

*(During the next passage, Jesus walks from the back
with a towel and a basin and as he nears the front,
Peter rises;*

Jesus stands motionless while Peter speaks and
during the first part of the Narrator's next speech)

During supper, Jesus, well aware
that the Father had entrusted everything to him
and that he had come from God
and was going back to God,
rose from the table,
laid aside his garments
and taking a towel, tied it round him.
Then he poured water into a basin
and began to wash the disciples' feet
and to wipe them with the towel.

Peter: You're not going to wash my feet.
You're not going to wash my feet!
I mean it and I won't let you.
It's not your job, such dirty work.
It's not your place to be seen doing
what masters love and servants loathe.
And I – we – have come to call you master;
and you – *you* want to be our servant!
Oh, how humiliating!

You are the one we call our Lord.
You are the one on whose own word
all our words hang.

You are the one we'll always follow,
the one we'll never reject,
never betray,
never deny.

Why empty yourself of dignity
to go down on the ground like a slave?
If you're down on your knees
won't the world walk on by,
thinking you feeble and weak?
Why not rule from the sky,
stretch your arms round the world,
not my ankles?

You're not going to wash my feet.
You're not going to wash my ...

Narrator: *(Interrupting)*

Peter,
this is what he must do.
And this is what you must let him do.
To prevent it ...
is to pretend to be perfect,
and you are in need of as much washing as us all.

(Pause while Jesus approaches and Peter sits. The
following words are said as water can be heard
washing Peter's feet)

This, whom you call "servant," is your Lord.
To be the Lord means to be the servant;
to do the dirty work
and to do it in love.

And that is very costly, although you count it
    stupid.
For a good world,
a man may lay down his life with pride;
but for a bad world
and for people who reject, betray, deny,
it is much harder.

His power is in his weakness.
And you may not know that today,
and you will not think it tomorrow,
when from a cross,
against the sky,
he hangs helpless.

But this is the way the world is transformed ...
by loving the unlovely,
by dying for the lifeless,
by forgiving those, like you,
whose hearts are too stubborn to see
what they are
or know who he is.

Be still,
and let your feet be washed
and let your mouth be closed.

Think not always to act,
always to speak.
But first let your Lord do for you
what you must do for each other.

(Music, possibly a hymn, during which the chancel is
prepared for the celebration of Holy Communion)

The Lord is my shepherd
Holy Week meditation 2

Jesus quoted from the PSALMS throughout his life; words from them were among the last words on his lips. But they also foreshadow many of the events of the Passion, none perhaps as remarkably as PSALM 23. In this, many of the specific incidents of Jesus' final days, and indeed his state of mind, are evoked. This meditation, with the help of some symbols, merely seeks to illustrate these. It is particularly poignant when read on Maundy Thursday.

Personnel: **Narrator**
                 Jesus
                 Peter
                 Voice
                 Judas

Narrator: The Lord is my Shepherd ...

Jesus: I am the good shepherd,
                  and I know my sheep
                  and my sheep know me;
                  and I am willing to lay down my life for them.

Narrator: He makes me lie down in green pastures,
                  he leads me to water where I may rest;
                  he revives my spirit.

                  (Basin and towel placed centrally)

Peter: Jesus, never at any time are you going to wash my feet!

Jesus: Peter, if I don't wash your feet,
                  you will no longer be my disciple.

Peter: Then don't just wash my feet, Lord;
                  wash my head and hands as well.

Narrator:	For his name's sake, he guides me in the right paths.
	(Candle placed centrally)
Jesus:	I am the way and the truth and the life: no one comes to the Father except by me.
Narrator:	Even if I were to walk through a valley of deepest darkness ...
Voice:	Golgotha.
Narrator:	Even if I were to walk through a valley ...
Voice:	Gethsemane.
Narrator:	Even if I were to walk ...
Voice:	They stripped him and whipped him and spat upon him and hit him over the head and led him out ...
Jesus:	I will fear no harm, for you are with me; your staff and crook strengthen me.
Narrator:	You spread a table before me in the presence of my enemies.
	(Bread and wine placed centrally)
Narrator:	You spread a table before me in the presence of my enemies.
Jesus:	One of you sitting here is going to betray me.
Peter:	Lord, is it me?
	(Silence)
Judas:	Lord, is it me?
Jesus:	Do what you have to do, Judas. But do it quickly.

Narrator: You have richly bathed my head with oil.

(Perfume placed centrally by a woman)

Judas: It's a waste!
It could have been sold for a fortune,
and the money given to the poor.

Jesus: You'll always have the poor with you
but you won't always have me.
What this woman has done
was to prepare me for my burial,
ahead of time.
She has done something fine and beautiful.

Narrator: You have richly bathed my head with oil
and my cup runs over.

Jesus: Father, take away this cup of suffering from me.
It is possible for you to do that.
Nevertheless, let it be not what I want,
but what you want.

Narrator: Goodness and love unfailing ...
these will follow me all the days of my life.

Peter: Lord, where are you going?

Jesus: Where I am going, you cannot, for now, come.
But one day you will.

Narrator: And I shall live in the house of the Lord
all the days of my life.

Jesus: In my Father's house are many rooms.
I am going there to prepare a place for you.
And if I go, I will come back
and take you to myself,
so that where I am, you may be also.

Sit here while I pray
Holy Week reading 5

This is the prayer of Jesus in the Garden, slightly paraphrased in places. It may be used at the end of a Maundy Thursday service with the intention of allowing the congregation to hear what the disciples heard in Gethsemane ... Jesus praying for them. It is best read slowly, though not over-dramatically.

Sit here while I pray.
The sorrow in my heart is so great,
it almost crushes me.
Stay here and keep watch with me.

Father, I have shown your glory on earth;
I have finished the work you gave me.

I have given my disciples your message
and the world ... it hated them.

Yet I don't pray
that they may be taken out of the world.
I pray that they may be kept from evil.

(Sound of snoring)

Sleeping, Peter?
Can you not even keep awake for an hour?

Father, I pray not only for my friends,
but for all who believe their words.

I pray that they may be one,
just as you and I are one.

Father, the world does not know you,
but I know you and they know you.

So that the world may believe

that you sent me,
may they be one...
may they be one.

(Sound of snoring)

Peter, keep watch and pray.
Don't be drawn by temptation.
The spirit is willing,
but, oh, the flesh ...
the flesh is weak.

Father, if it is possible...

Father, if it is possible...

take away this cup of suffering from me...

take away this cup of suffering from me...

but let it not be what I want.

Let it be what you want.

(Sound of snoring)

Are you still sleeping?
Are you still taking your ease?
The hour has come for the Son of Man
to be handed over to sinful people.
Get up, let us go!
Look, here comes the one who is to betray me...

↑ Stripping the church
Holy Week symbolic action 4

As previously discussed in MAUNDY THURSDAY (i) on page 100, the scriptural passage of Psalm 22 may be read at the end of a Maundy Thursday service.

It may be read by a leader, with the congregation responding, or by left and right sides of the congregation alternately. As this happens, the church or room may be stripped of all decoration (cloth, hangings, flowers) reminding us of how all that delighted our Lord, including his friends, were taken from him. Larger objects symbolizing God's grace which are less easy to carry out (communion table, font, lectern) may be covered by black cloth or a similar material. In addition, it may be possible and appropriate as part of the stripping process to progressively extinguish the lighting, particularly if there are candles or more than one electric light. Thus, towards the end of the reading people may be unable to see to read and the sound may tail off to a few or merely one voice reading as the darkness descends.

Rehearsal of both stripping the decoration and extinguishing the lights is very important.

While it need not be extensively choreographed, the manner of movement needs to be quietly deliberate to underscore the drama of the text; the relative speed at which people move should also have a quiet urgency, paced to ensure that all the artifacts to be removed have been by the third or fourth last verse. The church strippers should also be clear about what it is they take away each time they move, from where and to where this has to be taken.

Pace is particularly important for the lights, as these need to go out gradually, with the last one being extinguished at the point that the last lines are spoken. Where candles rather than electric lights are used, two or three people may need to be employed. In the case of electric light it is always important to check which switches turn off which lights, particularly if these switches are located in more than one place. The order in which the lights go off will also affect which parts of the church will be able to see and thus be able to read for longest.

To heighten the sense of desolation and loss that is the characteristic of the next couple of days, some congregations will refrain from accompanying singing with any musical instrumentation. This parallels the stripping of all beautiful artifacts from the church. Where there is a larger immovable musical instrument, such as a piano or organ, this may be covered by black cloth in the same way as the communion table or font.

Personnel: **Leader**
Church strippers
Light extinguisher(s)

Leader: My God, my God, why have you forsaken me?
I have cried desparately for help,
but still it does not come.

ALL: DURING THE DAY, I CALL TO YOU, O GOD,
BUT YOU DO NOT ANSWER.
I CALL AT NIGHT, BUT GET NO REST.

Leader: Yet you are the one enthroned as the Holy One,
you are the one whom Israel praises.

ALL: OUR ANCESTORS PUT THEIR TRUST IN YOU;
THEY TRUSTED YOU AND YOU SAVED THEM.

Leader: They called to you and escaped from danger;
they trusted you and were not disappointed.

ALL: BUT I AM NO LONGER A MAN: I AM A WORM;
I AM DESPISED AND SCORNED BY EVERYONE.

Leader: All who see me, jeer at me;
they stick out their tongues and shake their heads.

ALL: "YOU RELIED ON THE LORD, WHY DOESN'T HE SAVE
YOU?
IF THE LORD LIKES YOU, WHY DOESN'T HE HELP
YOU?"

Leader: It was you who brought me safely through birth,
and when I was a baby, you kept me safe.

ALL: I HAVE RELIED ON YOU SINCE THE DAY I WAS
BORN,

AND YOU HAVE ALWAYS BEEN MY GOD.

Leader: Do not stay away from me!
Trouble is near and there is no one to help.

ALL: MANY ENEMIES SURROUND ME LIKE BULLS,
LIKE FIERCE BULLS FROM THE LAND OF BASHAN.

Leader: They open their mouths like lions,
roaring and tearing at me.

ALL: MY STRENGTH IS GONE
LIKE WATER SPILT ON THE GROUND.
MY BONES ARE OUT OF JOINT,
MY HEART IS LIKE MELTED WAX.

Leader: My throat is dry as dust, my tongue sticks to my
mouth.
You have left me for dead in the dust.

ALL: A GANG OF EVIL MEN SURROUNDS ME.
LIKE DOGS, THEY CLOSE IN ON ME,
TEARING MY HANDS AND FEET.

Leader: O Lord, don't stay away from me!
Come quickly to my rescue.

ALL: SAVE ME FROM THE SWORD;
SAVE MY LIFE FROM THESE DOGS.

Leader: Rescue me from these lions.
I am helpless before these wild bulls.

ALL: I WILL TELL MY PEOPLE WHAT YOU HAVE DONE.
I WILL PRAISE YOU IN THE ASSEMBLY.

Leader: Praise him, you descendants of Jacob!
Worship him you people of Israel!

ALL: HE DOES NOT NEGLECT THE POOR:
HE ANSWERS WHEN THEY CALL FOR HELP.

Leader: Future generations will serve him;
and will speak of the Lord to those following them.

ALL: PEOPLE NOT YET BORN WILL BE TOLD:
"THE LORD SAVES HIS PEOPLE."

Leader: ... I will strike the shepherd
and the sheep will be scattered ...

It was on the Thursday
Holy Week reading 6

This reading was originally printed as part of a larger piece consisting of the other IT WAS ON ... readings found in this book. It was primarily intended to be read by people on their own, as personal preparation for a series of workshops and reflections during Holy Week.

Alternatively, it may be read in a similar way, but on its own on the Thursday of Holy Week.

It was on the Thursday
that he became valuable.

He hadn't anything to sell ...
not since leaving his hammer and saw three years
    earlier.
Needless to say,
he could build a set of trestles
or hang a couple of shelves at the drop of a hat,
no bother at all.

But he wasn't into making things.
Not now.

He was into...
well ... talking, I suppose.
And listening
and healing
and forgiving
and encouraging ...
all the things for which there's no pay
and the job center has no advertisements.

So his work wasn't worth much.
Nor, indeed, was he.
For, not being well dressed
or well heeled or well connected,
he wouldn't have attracted many ticket holders

had he been put up for raffle.
But he had a novelty value ...
like the elephant man or the fat lady
or the midget at the circus.
Put him on a stage and he might be interesting to
    look at.
Sell him to the circus
with the promise of some tricks
and there could be some money in it.

It was on the Thursday
that he became valuable.

↑ Good Friday
Holy Week symbolic action 5

On Iona, the remembrance of Jesus' Passion is in three stages and it happens (ideally) between 12 noon and 3:00 pm, the traditional time attributed to his crucifixion and death.

a) Stations of the Cross
This has an ancient pedigree and should be accessible for people of all traditions.

On Iona, those present for Holy Week are invited to do one of three things:

i) take a station and physically depict it in an art form;
ii) write a brief two-minute meditation which may be read at each station;
iii) in association with (ii), write a brief penitential or intercessory prayer.

Only those stations leading up to Christ being crucified and his death, as indicated below, are used:

1. Jesus is condemned to death
2. Jesus takes up his cross
3. Jesus falls for the first time
4. Jesus meets his mother
5. Simon of Cyrene is forced to carry the cross
6. Veronica wipes the face of Jesus
7. Jesus falls a second time
8. Jesus meets the women of Jerusalem
9. Jesus falls a third time
10. Jesus is stripped of his garments
11. Jesus is nailed to the cross
12. Jesus dies on the cross

At one time, the stations were set up in the Abbey Church. More recently they have been erected outside, along the half-mile walk from the shore to the Abbey. This has resulted in many more people joining the procession. There is also a greater feeling of journeying with Christ than can happen in a small worship area.

To aid movement, a large wooden cross may be carried between stations and a chant sung as people move on. BEHOLD THE LAMB OF GOD or WONDER AND STARE (from the COME ALL YOU PEOPLE collection) are suitable. They need not be sung continuously if there is a fair distance between stations.

The last station should be in the center of the church, where the cross should be set upright.

b) Words from the Cross
If the stations take about an hour, the Seven Words from the Cross are given the next hour and a half until 2:30 pm. The time is divided into seven sections and seven individuals are asked to prepare a meditation no longer than 5 minutes which should end with a prayer. By doing this rather than having a cleric "preach the Passion" more people are involved.

There is no singing and it may be that up to 15 minutes of silence may happen between the meditations, each of which begins with a statement of the appropriate word from the cross:

> Father, forgive them. They do not know what they are doing.
>
> Today you will be with me in paradise.
>
> Mother, there is your son.
>
> My God, my God, why have you forsaken me?
>
> I am thirsty.
>
> It is finished.
>
> Father, into your hands I commit my spirit.

SEVEN WORDS FROM THE CROSS on page 152 is a set of prayers which may be used at this time.

c) Penitential Rite
At 2:30 pm a bell is rung and people assemble for the penitential rite.

Everyone in the church should have access to a pencil and to a small piece of paper which is either blank or on which is written words such as:

> Before God and in the face of the cross
> I confess these sins which burden me,

I regret the hurt they have caused God,
the people of God and my own self,
and I ask God, in his mercy, to forgive me.

Beside the cross should be a metal bucket or other large non-flammable receptacle and in front of it a large candle.

The leader of worship should briefly introduce the rite, asking people to recall that in their lives which needs to be confessed and forgiven. Such things may be written down on the paper and, as people wish, they can come forward, kneel before the cross, set fire to the paper and leave it to burn out in the bucket.

At 3:00 pm the leader then may say these or other similar words:

After three hours on the cross,
our Lord committed himself to God and died.

But he did not do that
before he had asked forgiveness
on all those who had done him wrong.

So now in the face of the cross,
I declare, to all who are truly penitent,
these gracious words of God:

"Your sins are forgiven."

So go in peace
in the knowledge
and in the hope of eternal life,
which are ours
through the promise of Jesus Christ our Lord.
AMEN.

d) Good Friday Evening
On Iona, the Good Friday evening worship does not happen in one venue, but in several. To recall the scattering of the disciples, five or six rooms, chapels or other small gathering places are made available, lit only by candlelight. In each place there is a worship leader and someone to start unaccompanied singing.

WHEN JESUS DIED, on page 166, is an example of this kind of simple and short evening prayer.

They went out and followed him
Holy Week reading 7

Suitable for use during a Good Friday service, this reading looks back on the events of the previous 24 hours in Jesus' life.

They went out and followed him,
those who had sat with him at the table.
He led them to a garden
where he prayed while they slept,
        prayed while they slept,
        prayed while they slept.

He was kissed,
and because he was kissed he was arrested,
and when he was arrested, his friends fled,
some to go into hiding,
one to stand beside a bonfire
and say I never knew him,
        I never knew him,
        I never knew him ... until a cock crowed.

He was brought before the religious authorities
and accused of the sin of blasphemy
and of threatening insurrection.
Having no power to deal with him,
they handed him over to the state governor,
who listened to the accusations
and then asked the accused:
        what have you to say?
        what have you to say?
        what have you to say?
... to which the response was silence.

He had said it all.

He was not found to be guilty of any criminal
    charges,
but because he was an embarrassment,

it was decided
that his own people should determine his fate.
This they did by shouting,
        crucify him!
        crucify him!
        crucify him!

He was cursed and spat on,
whipped and humiliated.
And on his shoulders a gift was placed,
which he accepted with grace.
Under the weight of this gift,
he stumbled and fell
    stumbled and fell
    stumbled and fell ...
all the way to Calvary.

On top of a garbage dump,
he was nailed to a cross of wood
and left to die,
while soldiers gambled,
critics joked,
religious leaders smiled with satisfaction
and his mother watched and waited,
            watched and waited,
            watched and waited ...
until in the end she saw a sign of the beginning.

The trials
Holy Week script 3

Jesus was not merely tried before Pilate, the political authority. He was first tried before the Sanhedrin, the Jewish religious court.

This script allows both trials to be represented. It is not literal nor does it exhaust the possibilities of dramatizing the courtroom scenes, but it attempts to make clear (a) that Jesus was sent to his death by religious people, (b) that false accusations were framed against him, and (c) that in fulfillment of prophecy he had committed no sin nor did he defend himself with anything other than the eloquence of silence.

A traditional reformed church building with a high pulpit and a reading desk or lectern is ideally suited for the script.

Pilate should be out of sight either in a side balcony or in the pulpit. Caiaphas needs to occupy a slightly less elevated central position ... the pulpit or a raised dais on which an imposing chair may be positioned. The witnesses can read from a lectern, angled so that their voices are projected to the congregation. Alternatively, they might be placed sitting among the congregation. The narrator reads from the back and Jesus, who has only one line, can either stand at the back or stand in the middle of the center aisle.

Caiaphas and Pilate can be dressed in some kind of religious or civic garb and Jesus, dressed in ordinary clothes, may have his hands tied behind his back.

The introductory passage to be read by the worship leader may be omitted or amended as desired.

Personnel: **Leader**
Narrator
Caiaphas, *high priest*
Shabeth, *an informer*
Jolbad, *an informer*
Annas, *father-in-law of Caiaphas*
Pilate
Jesus
A, *one of the crowd*
B, *one of the crowd*
C, *one of the crowd*

Leader: We have come on this night/day to remember,
to remember how the King of Heaven
was, on earth, betrayed, rejected
and sent to his death by religious people
who thought they were doing the right thing.

We have come knowing that we ourselves
would have done the same.

But we believe,
and in the life of Christ we see,
that the love of God is greater than the sin of the
    world.

That is the hope which takes us
through the suffering and death of Jesus
to the joy of his resurrection.

Narrator: He grew up before the Lord like a young plant
whose roots are in dry ground:
he had no beauty, no majesty to draw our eyes,
no grace to make us delight in him;
his form, disfigured,
lost all likeness of a man,
his beauty changed beyond all recognition.

He was despised, he shrank from the sight of
    people,
tormented and humbled by suffering.
We despised him, we held him of no account,
a thing from which people turn away their eyes.

Yet he himself bore our sufferings;
our torments he endured
while we thought he was punished by God,
struck down by disease and misery.

We had all strayed like sheep:
each of us had gone our own way.
But the Lord laid on him the guilt of us all.

Caiaphas: *(Stands)*
As high priest,
I am the official guardian
of our traditional and orthodox religion.

It is my duty to investigate heresies

and to discipline heretics
and any other who would pervert our faith.

I have been summoned this night/day
to investigate complaints against one,
Jesus,
from the town of Nazareth in Galilee.
So let me hear the accusations.
Who are the witnesses for the prosecution?

(Shabeth goes to the lectern)

Shabeth: I am one, sir.

Caiaphas: Who are you?

Shabeth: My name is Shabeth.
I am a friend of Annas, your father-in-law.
I change foreign currency for visitors to our city.

Caiaphas: And what have you to say?

Shabeth: I have it here.
(Brings out a paper)

I wrote it down.

Caiaphas: Why?

Shabeth: In case I forgot it.
I want to get it right.
He ... that man ...
(Points)
Jesus ...
he said he would destroy the Temple.

Caiaphas: What?

Shabeth: He said he would pull down the Temple ...
destroy it.

Caiaphas: Did you hear him say that?

Shabeth: Eh ... no ...
that is ... not personally.
But I know someone who did
and they told me
and I told Annas

and that's why I'm here.

Caiaphas: And how exactly was he going to destroy the
Temple?

Shabeth: I don't know ...
but I've a good idea.

A lot of people know him;
a lot of people listen to him;
a lot of people follow him.
If they get hysterical ... they'll do anything.

Caiaphas: Who are these people?

Shabeth: The lower classes, sir ...
the crowds ...
the rabble ...

Caiaphas: Anything else?

Shabeth: Well ...
there was a rumor about him
and a servant woman from Bethany.
I'm not one for gossip,
but I wouldn't be surprised if it were true.

Caiaphas: *(Looks at Shabeth, nods and waves him down)*
Be seated.
Now who else?
Who else has information?

(Jolbad goes to the lectern)

Jolbad: Me, sir.
I have information.

Caiaphas: Who are you?

Jolbad: My name is Jolbad.
I am a friend of Annas, your father-in-law,
and I'm a cleaner in the Temple.

Caiaphas: And what have you to say?

Jolbad: Here it is.
I have it here.

(Brings a paper out)

I also wrote it down.
I did not want to forget.

Yes,
(Looks over it)
it says ...

That man ...
eh ... Jesus ...
he said he would build another Temple.

Caiaphas: Build another Temple?

Jolbad: Yes ... in three days.

Caiaphas: Do you expect me to believe that?

Jolbad: It's true, sir.
That's what he said.

Caiaphas: Did you hear him say it?

Jolbad: Well, yes ... and no ...
You see, I was standing on the edge of the crowd.
I could not hear everything.
I could only make out some words now and then.
So I asked a man who was standing closer
and that's what he told me.

Caiaphas: And you believed that man?

Jolbad: Yes, of course.
He ... Jesus, that is ...
he does tricks.
He does magic tricks;
he does tricks with fish and bread;
he does tricks with trees;
he threatens to move mountains and ruin our
   landscape.

Personally, I think he works for the devil.

He will build another Temple in three days if he
   wants to.
But it will be the temple of Satan.

Caiaphas:	Did he say that?
Jolbad:	Does he have to? Isn't it obvious, sir?
Caiaphas:	Anything else?
Jolbad:	Yes. I don't know if I should say this in such a place, but ... he talks to prostitutes. Oh, yes. I know it for a fact. I've seen the kind of company he keeps.
Caiaphas:	*(Waves him down)* Take your seat. Who else?
Annas:	There's me. *(Annas goes to the lectern)*
Caiaphas:	Your name please.
Annas:	I am Annas. I am your father-in-law. I have much to do with our religion, like you, and I have much to say about this man. *(Opens his script)* Firstly, you have heard what he said about the Temple. I admit the information is not clear, but it is enough surely to convince you that he is a threat to the life of our beloved institution. Secondly, he is a threat ... to our national security. We live at peace under the Roman government. We pay our taxes, we behave responsibly; we gain the benefits of Roman civilization. We respect Pilate, our Governor; we respect Caesar, our Emperor,

although we don't worship him as others do.
We value the peace and the progress
we have in our country.

And then along comes this man
questioning Caesar's authority,
saying to the people:
"Give to Caesar what belongs to him"
... these, more or less, are his words.

Now, what have you that belongs to Caesar,
and what have I?
Do we have Caesar's furniture?
        Caesar's palaces?
        Caesar's slaves?
        Caesar's books?
Of course not.

The conclusion, as I understand it,
is that because we have nothing belonging to
  Caesar,
we should forget about him.

But let us forget about Caesar for one minute
and he will not forget us.

No ... we will suffer for our lack of memory.

The man is a nationalist of the worst variety,
for he is a threat to our nation's peace.

And thirdly ...
he is a threat to our religion
for he claims to be the Messiah.

(Pointing)
This ... this tradesman
has been tricking the faithful of our religion,
turning their minds away from the true worship,
encouraging them to believe
that he and his philosophies were sent from God.

This ... this tradesman
and his twelve ignorant companions
have been encouraging immoral practices,
breaking the law of the Sabbath,

questioning the authority of the priests,
preaching heresy ...

Caiaphas: (Suddenly interrupting)
Stop ...
stop ...

(He rises and moves angrily to the front)
Is this true?
Is this all true?
Are you the Messiah?

(Silence)

Speak, man!!!

Jesus: These are your words.

Caiaphas: These are my words?
These are your words!
These words are blasphemy.

Caiaphas: (Yells) Pilate!

(Caiaphas now goes to the lectern)

Pilate: (Naively) Yes, Caiaphas?

Caiaphas: Your excellency,
this is the day before our holy celebrations,
our Passover.

On this day our nation rids itself
of anything which is unclean or foul.
So, on this day, I bring you this foul man.

I have no authority
to prescribe the punishment
which is most fitting.
But in your hands there lies the power
to deal with him as he deserves.

Pilate: Why?
What has he done?

Caiaphas: Three things ...

He is a threat to our nation and our religion
for he questions and breaks our rules of faith.

He has opposed the payment of taxes to Caesar
and sets himself up as a rival power.

He claims to be a King.
He says that he is our Messiah.
As high priest, I know he is not.

But I fear the wickedness that may follow
if this man is left at liberty.

Pilate: Is that him?

Caiaphas: That is him.
His name is Jesus.

Pilate: Your name is Jesus ...
You've heard what has been said against you,
so what do you say in your defense?

(Silence)

I repeat,
you've heard what has been said against you,
now what do you say in your defense?

(Silence)

Look here, man ...
your life is at risk.
Are you not going to defend yourself?

(Silence. Pilate becomes exasperated)

Let me make myself clear ...
you have been brought to me on three charges.
These charges are made by your religious
    authorities.
Now I'm not a Jew;
I don't worship your God;
religious matters don't even interest me.

But because the Jews have no courts of their own,
I have to administer justice for them.

If this were an ordinary trial,
if you had stolen some sheep
or killed a man,
I would know what to do.

But religious heretics and Jewish messiahs
only confuse me.

I have no complaints about you
from the police or the army,
only from your religious leaders.
In their eyes, not mine,
you are guilty.
If you can convince me otherwise
I am prepared to let you go.

Now, what have you to say?

(Silence)

Speak, man!
What have you got to say?

(Silence, then Pilate turns to the Jews)

Pilate: Under Roman law,
I cannot find this man guilty.
But if he has caused trouble to you
and to your establishment,
I am prepared to have him flogged
and set free.

A: No! Barabbas!
Give us Barabbas!

B: No! Barabbas!

C: No! Barabbas!

Pilate: Then what am I to do with this man?

A: Crucify him!

B: Crucify him!

C: Crucify him!

Pilate: Crucify your ... King?

A, B & C: *(All speaking at one time)*
HE IS NOT OUR KING!
WHO SAYS HE'S OUR KING?
RUBBISH!
LIES, LIES, LIES!

Caiaphas: He is not our King!
Caesar is!
And you ... are Caesar's delegate.

Pilate: Then,
if he must be crucified,
he must be crucified.

In my hands
lies the authority for his death,
but in your hands,
I leave the responsibility.

(Pilate and Caiaphas remain motionless and look at the congregation. A drum beat may start.)

Narrator: He was afflicted;
he submitted to being struck down
and did not open his mouth.
He was led like a sheep to the slaughter,
like a ewe that is dumb before her shearers.

Without protection,
without justice,
he was taken away
and who gave a thought to his fate?
He was cut off from the world of the living,
put to death for the people's sin.
He was given a grave with the wicked,
a burial place among the rubbish of humanity,
though he had done nothing wrong,
and said nothing which was untrue.

(Characters leave in silence. The drumbeat stops.)

Savior of the world
Holy Week prayer 2

A prayer addressed to Jesus on the cross while he is still alive, which admits our complicity in his fate.

Savior of the world,
what have you done to deserve this?
And what have we done to deserve you?

Strung up between criminals,
cursed and spat upon,
you wait for death,
and look for us,
for us whose sin has crucified you.

To the mystery of undeserved suffering,
you bring the deeper mystery of unmerited love.

Forgive us for not knowing what we have done;
open our eyes to what we are doing now,
as, through wood and nails,
you disempower our depravity
and transform us by your grace.
AMEN.

Voices from the crowd
Holy Week meditation 3

The six monologues which follow on pages 143–151 formed the basis of a Holy Week reflection on Christ on the cross. They were first used on Good Friday at an ecumenical evening service and they are the product of a group Bible study. Essentially, people were asked to reflect on the biblical characters who saw Jesus on the way to the cross: their physical appearance, likes and dislikes of the character and what, if anything, they would want to say to Jesus as he passed by. The purpose is to enable reflection by allowing the characters who met Jesus to speak.

Although they can be used on their own, they originally formed the main part of a service, preceded by a call to worship and followed by a penitential prayer with symbolic action. A description of this, along with the penitential prayer, can be found on page 161, LAYING OUR BURDEN DOWN.

The scripts require a little rehearsal, although the characters should still have their words in front of them.

Ideally, the place of worship should have movable seating. If so, arrange the chairs in a classical "choir" formation, that is, in rows on two sides facing inwards to the center, rather than towards the chancel or altar area. Try to ensure gaps every six or eight chairs to allow people to move in and out to make the symbolic action LAYING OUR BURDEN DOWN, if used.

The corridor or middle aisle between should be broad enough for a person carrying a substantial wooden cross (at least 6 feet high) to move down, towards the altar or chancel area. This helps provide a focus for people's attention.

Each of the six characters should sit at the back of the assembly, next to the wall for better acoustic projection. Place them on both sides at regular intervals along the length of the seating.

When the reader begins the first script, the person carrying the cross starts moving and stops in the middle aisle in line with the character who is about to speak.

At the conclusion of each script, the short biblical responses below are read, followed by a short song or chant, e.g., a verse of WERE YOU THERE WHEN THEY CRUCIFIED MY LORD? or BEHOLD THE LAMB OF GOD. As this is sung the cross moves on into line with the next character who is about to speak. This continues until, after the last reading, the biblical responses and the closing passage shown below, the cross is placed upright on the chancel or altar area.

Personnel: **Leader**
Narrator
Larry, *the owner of the upper room*
Rachel, *a servant girl*
Barabbas, *the criminal*
Simon, *the cross carrier*
Cato, *a soldier*
Mary, *mother of Jesus*

Larry, the owner of the upper room

Narrator: On the day he was betrayed,
Jesus told his disciples to go
to a certain man in the city
with this message:
"My appointed time is near;
I will keep the Passover with my disciples
at your house."

Larry: I am that man,
my name is Larry;
and last night he came to my house.

It's next to a builder's yard on the south side.
It has a big front room
and I got it ready for him.

I had met him before;
he had challenged me once
about how much money I had
and how little of it I gave away.

He taught me how to be generous.
That's why I was eager to give him the room,
to say, "It's all yours, Jesus."

But what can I say now?

Jesus,
you told me to give away everything
and take up my cross.

Maybe if I had done that,
maybe if all of us had done that,
you wouldn't be strung up,
crucified by people
who find you too threatening.

We all could have earned less
and loved more,
and I could have taken you more seriously.

Because I stood back and did nothing,
I helped you onto the cross
and I am deeply,
deeply sorry.

(The following responses are read after each of the six scripts.)

Leader: He was wounded for our sins,
he was crushed by our wrongdoing.

ALL: WE HAD ALL STRAYED LIKE SHEEP.
WE HAD ALL GONE OUR OWN WAY.

Leader: But the Lord laid on him the guilt of us all.

(Sung response)

Rachel, a servant girl

Narrator: After his arrest at Gethsemane,
Jesus was taken to the high priest's house.
It was early in the morning.

Peter followed at a distance
and then warmed himself
at a fire in the courtyard.

He was sitting there when a servant girl confronted
    him.

Rachel: I am that girl
           and my name is Rachel.
           I work in the priest's house
           so I know everything about everybody.
           That's why I recognized Peter.
           I'd seen him with Jesus.

           But I'd never seen anything
           like what happened this morning.

           I arrived at my usual time ...
           about five o'clock.

           I was going to start cleaning the main hall,
           but I couldn't get near it.
           The place was packed;
           everybody was shouting.
           It was a madhouse.

           I couldn't say a thing.
           What can I say now?

                 Jesus,
                 you don't deserve any of this.

                 The men who hit you and swore at you
                 might call themselves religious,
                 but they're just scum,
                 a pack of liars all of them.

                 They were jealous of you
                 because people listened to you,
                 because you said that God loved the poor,
                 because you let us see that God could smile
                 and heal and even cry;
                 while all they could do
                 was criticize and condemn people.

                 I wish I had spoken up this morning, Jesus.
                 I wish I had shouted
                 that you were a good man.
                 I wish I had told them
                 that you had healed my little sister.

                 I'm sorry, Jesus,

that in the face of wicked men,
I never put in a good word for you.

Barabbas, the criminal

Narrator: When Jesus appeared before Pilate,
Pilate realized he was innocent.
Because he was the Governor,
he had a custom at the Passover of releasing a
    prisoner,
who could be chosen by the crowd.

But the chief priests and elders
had infiltrated the crowd
and persuaded them to ask for Barabbas,
so that Jesus would be put to death.

Barabbas: And I'm Barabbas
and I'm a free man,
though by rights,
I should be hanging on a cross.

Everybody knows me
and knows what I've done
and it's more than keeping pigeons near the railway
    line.

I was up on a murder charge
and two of grievous bodily harm
with intent to kill.
I've mugged more people
than Pilate's had hot breakfasts.

So it was a great surprise to me
to be sitting on Death Row
and hear the chant going up,
"Barabbas... Barabbas ..."
as if I was a film star.

I walked past Jesus' cell on the way out.
I never said anything then.
What can I say now?

Jesus,
either you're out of your mind
or they're out of theirs.

You'd done nothing wrong,
I'd done nothing right,
but they chose me.

You came to the wrong place,
at the wrong time
and your face didn't fit.
That's why they went for you.

They say,
that when you landed up
in front of the Governor,
you never said a word.

If that had been me,
I'd have lied until I was blue in the face.
But that's maybe
because I have plenty to lie about.

Well, now I've got something to be straight
   about:
you've taken my place.
I'm in your debt
and always will be.

Simon, the cross carrier

Narrator: The soldiers of the Governor took Jesus to his
         residence.
         There they collected the whole company around
            him.
         They stripped him
         and dressed him in a scarlet cloak;
         they plaited a crown of thorns
         and put it on his head,
         and placed a stick in his right hand.

         Falling on their knees before him,
         they jeered at him and shouted,
         "Hail, King of the Jews!"
         They spat on him
         and used sticks to beat him on the head.

         When they had finished mocking him,
         they stripped him of the cloak

and dressed him in his own clothes.

Then they led him away to be crucified.
On their way out,
they met a man from Cyrene,
Simon by name,
and they compelled him to carry Jesus' cross.

Simon: I am Simon.
I come from Cyrene
and I would not have been in Jerusalem today
if it had not been for my business.
I'm a traveler.

And perhaps
I would not have been asked to carry the cross
if my color was not so obvious.

"You ... nigger ... come here!"
they shouted;
and what can a black man say
in a crowd of white people?

Jesus,
I don't know what all this is about.

I've never seen such degrading cruelty
and the reason is beyond my
        understanding.

What did you do
to make people hate you?
What did you do
to get hung on a cross?

You never robbed a bank.
You never mugged innocent people.
You never raped women,
        swindled money,
        planned an armed struggle,
        or committed treason.

Most people say you were a holy man,
some say you were God's son.
If this is the case,
why are religious people persecuting you?

Cato, a soldier

Narrator: When they reached the place called the Skull,
they crucified him with two criminals,
one on his left, the other on his right.

Jesus said, "Father, forgive them
for they don't know what they're doing."

The soldiers divided up his clothes
by gambling for them.
The people stood looking up;
the rulers jeered at him.

Then the soldiers joined in the mockery
and came forward offering him vinegar.

Cato: I'm the one who offered him the vinegar.
My name is Cato.

I just happened to be on execution duty.
We all take our turn.
None of us like it.
You have to deal with women screaming,
children bawling
and the odd drunk
who wants to challenge the victim to a fight.

Today was really unusual.
A lot of people just kept quiet.
The people who made the most noise
were the priests and elders.
It was the "important people"...
those who normally stay back from executions,
who were shouting abuse.
And I have to admit
that I was tempted to join in
... just in case they thought I was on his side.

What can I say now?

Jesus ...
I was only doing my job.
I know you've been framed.
I know you shouldn't be up there.
But I can't take you down.
I'm not my own boss.

Yet, this is a lame excuse.

I wonder how many other people
won't help you,
won't speak up for you,
let the worst happen to you,
and then say,
"It's not my fault.
It's got nothing to do with me.
I was only doing my job."

Mary, mother of Jesus

Narrator: Near the cross on which Jesus hung,
his mother was standing
with his sister and another woman.

Jesus saw his mother
and he saw the disciple he loved
standing near her.

He said to his mother,
"Mother ... there is your son."
And he said to his disciple,
"There is your mother."

Mary: And I am his mother.
I am Mary.

When he was a baby,
an old man told me
that one day sorrow would pierce my heart
like a sword.

This is that day
and my heart breaks
as I watch him
who put others before himself,
being put to death
before all the others.

What can I say?

Jesus,
when you were a boy

you once told me
you had to be about your Father's business.
If this is your Father's business
and it has led you to this cross,
may it soon be finished.
And may God
who put you into my hands
now take you into his.

(This closing passage is read after the sixth reading of the responses above.)

Narrator: After all the mocking,
    all the torture,
    all the pain
and in front of those who watched from the crowd,
Jesus said,
"It is finished."
Then he bowed his head
and gave up the spirit.

(As a song is sung, the cross may be placed in the center.)

Seven words from the cross
Holy Week prayer 3

This set of seven prayers may be used as part of a meditation on the seven words Jesus is recorded as speaking from the cross, as described in GOOD FRIDAY, page 125.

The words of Jesus which begin each section are ideally spoken by a reader, although if necessary the leader may read them, pausing before continuing with the prayer.

Personnel: **Reader**
Leader

Reader: Father, forgive them.
They do not know what they are doing.

Leader: Before you die, Jesus Christ,
and the world goes into deep darkness,
take from our lives,
  from our souls,
  from our consciences
all that has offended you,
all that has hurt others,
and the intransigence
which has made us numb to the plight
of those whom we could help or heal.

Lamb of God,
you take away the sin of the world,
ALL: HAVE MERCY ON US.

Leader: Lamb of God,
you take away the sin of the world,
ALL: HAVE MERCY ON US.

Leader: Lamb of God,
you take away the sin of the world,
ALL: GRANT US YOUR PEACE.

Leader: On this day, at this time,
irrespective of our faith or lack of it,
we accept deeply in our hearts
the only words that can set us free:

your sins are forgiven,
your sins are forgiven.
AMEN.

Reader: Today you will be with me in paradise.

Leader: Lord Jesus, remember us
when you come into your kingdom.

Remember us,
not for our impressive accomplishments,
nor for the things
which we hope will appear in our obituaries.

Remember us,
not for the virtues we occasionally display
or for any credit
we think we have in our moral account.

Remember us,
as one of the criminal community
who hung at your side,
and if life will not let us be in paradise
with you today,
keep a place for us tomorrow.
AMEN.

Reader: Mother, there is your son ...

Leader: For our families,
where they are open, loving, supportive,
that their joy might be kept safe,
Lord, hear us,
ALL: LORD, GRACIOUSLY HEAR US.

Leader: For our families,
where they are tense, troubled, fragmented,
seething with suspicion,
that they may find a way through pain,
not a path away from it,

Lord, hear us,
ALL: LORD, GRACIOUSLY HEAR US.

Leader: For our churches,
where they risk welcoming the stranger,
where in language, hospitality,
evangelism and service,
they employ the imagination
rather than the rule book,
that they might be encouraged and surprised by
    joy,
Lord, hear us,
ALL: LORD, GRACIOUSLY HEAR US.

Leader: For our churches,
where they have become introverted,
suspicious of the stranger,
obsessed with dead rather than living stones,
suffocated by tradition,
that they might be redeemed
from the pawnshop of past glory
and renewed by the power of the Holy Spirit,
Lord, hear us,
ALL: LORD, GRACIOUSLY HEAR US.

Leader: For ourselves, in this place of worship,
surrounded by people
whose journey we have not traveled,
whose depth of faith we do not know,
whose potentials we cannot imagine,
that we might somehow know we belong to each
    other,
Lord, hear us,
ALL: LORD, GRACIOUSLY HEAR US.

Leader: And before you leave the cross
and we vacate this building,
if there is one of your family
for whom we should care more fondly,
direct our gaze to them,
as you turned Mary towards John.
AMEN.

Reader: My God, my God, why have you forsaken me?

Leader: Lord Jesus,
by your cry of desperate honesty,
rid us of superficial faith
which is afraid of the dark.

Not so that we might be justified pessimists,
but so that we might discover profound joy,
give us, when we need it,
the courage to doubt,
            to rage,
            to question,
            to rail against heaven
until we know we are heard.

We do not ask for easy answers
to hard times;
there are many who can offer these.

We ask for a sense of your solidarity,
that will be enough
to let us know
that we do not walk or cry alone;
that will enable us to go through the dark
and find light again in the morning.
AMEN.

Reader: I am thirsty.

Leader: You have made us for yourself.
We know it, even if we cannot name it.

We have had these bodies and these minds
long enough to learn to live
with our limitations.

Yet despite this,
something in us longs, yearns, thirsts
for something better,
    something greater
which we know is there.

Beautiful music ends
and we wish it could continue.

We embrace,

then refrain from embracing
and wish that we could be held forever.
We think deeply or feel deeply
and wish that this sense
of being caught up in living
would not be interrupted
by the mundane things of life.

We sense the disappointment
in dashed hopes
that deserve to be fulfilled,
in missed opportunities
which should have led to joy not frustration,
in people whose potential
has been buried or denied and deserves to flourish.

So much of life demands a resolution.

So thank you for this incompleteness,
thank you for this yearning,
thank you for this thirst.

Thank you for giving us enough of you
to want more,
and so to sense the fullness of eternity
within the limits of time.
AMEN.

Reader: It is finished.

Leader: Now, Lord Jesus,
you can let go of us.

You have convinced us of our sin
and you have forgiven it.
You have convinced us of your way
and have engaged us on it.
You have shown us a foretaste of heaven
and have made us members of its commonwealth.

You can let go of us now.

Having overcome the sin of the world,
death will be a small obstacle.

Just as you foretold
that you would be handed over to be crucified
and this has come true;
also as you foretold,
on the third day,
you will rise again.
And we will be your witnesses.
AMEN.

Reader: Father, into your hands I commit my spirit.

Leader: Go, silent friend,
your life has found its ending.
To dust returns your weary mortal frame.
God, who before birth,
called you into being,
now calls you back,
his accent still the same.

Lord Jesus, we let you go.

You cannot cling to life forever,
nor can we cling to a dying frame,
nor do we begrudge you
that peace which passes understanding
which you have promised us.

So go to heaven,
where you will welcome
those who die in your faith,
whose death, with your death, we remember.

Tell them that we love them,
        that we miss them,
        that they are not forgotten.

And cheered by the prospect of a day
when there will be no more death or parting,
and all shall be well
and all shall be one,
may they who have died before us
be among the first
to welcome us to heaven
where, with you enthroned in glory,

and in the company of the blessed virgin Mary
and all the saints,
we will share the everlasting feast of your family.

'Til then,
keep us in faith,
fill us with hope,
deepen us through love,
to the glory of your holy name.
AMEN.

It was on the Friday

Holy Week reading 8

This reading was originally printed as part of a larger piece consisting of the other IT WAS ON ... readings found in this book. It was primarily intended to be read by people on their own, as personal preparation for a series of workshops and reflections during Holy Week.

Alternatively, it may be read in a similar way, but on its own on the Friday of Holy Week.

It was on the Friday
that they ended it all.

Of course,
they didn't do it one by one.
They weren't brave enough.
All the stones at the one time
or no stones thrown at all.

They did it in crowds ...
in crowds where you can feel safe
and lose yourself
and shout things
you would never shout on your own,
and do things
you would never do
if you felt the camera was watching you.

It was a crowd in the church that did it,
and a crowd in the civil service that did it,
and a crowd in the street that did it,
and a crowd on the hill that did it.

And he said nothing.

He took the insults,
the bruises,
the spit on the face,

the thongs on the back,
the curses in the ears.
He took the sight of his friends turning away,
running away.

And he said nothing.

He let them do their worst
until their worst was done,
as on Friday they ended it all ...
and would have finished themselves
had he not cried,
"Father, forgive them ..."

And began the revolution.

↑ Laying our burden down
Holy Week symbolic action 6

This penitential prayer and symbolic action were originally used together with VOICES FROM THE CROWD on page 142. If these scripts are not used, the prayer should be preceded by a song during which a large wooden cross is brought in to a central position.

As the congregation enter, they should be given a small stone to hold during the service. When the song WE WILL LAY OUR BURDEN DOWN (from the LOVE FROM BELOW collection) is sung during the prayer, people may lay their stone down at the foot of the cross.

An appropriate song such as WHEN I SURVEY THE WONDROUS CROSS should be sung after the words of Jesus, which close the prayer.

Personnel: **Leader**
                  Reader

Leader: Could we all now take in our hands
the stone we have held during the service.

(Pause)

Stones are what people wanted to throw at Jesus
during his life;
stones are also what surrounded him in the tomb
and through them he pushed his way
back into life on the third day.

Could we,
as we remember our Lord's death
and see how he was crucified
by the action or the apathy
of people like ourselves,
remember that it was for our sins he died?

Let us remember the wrong things in our life
which burden us,

threaten each other
and offend God.

And after we have recognized
what these things are,
let us give them to God to take away.
For Jesus is the one
who said, "Give me your burdens,"
and Jesus is the Lamb of God
who takes away the sin of the world.

We'll be silent for a moment
and then we'll sing,
"We will lay our burden down."
And as we sing,
we can, if we want to,
take the stone, representing our burden,
and lay it at the foot of the cross.

*(Silence, then the song WE WILL LAY OUR BURDEN
DOWN – see next page – as people move to lay
their stones down in front of the cross)*

Leader: Let us listen to these words of Jesus,
spoken directly to us:

Reader: I am the good shepherd
and I know my sheep
and I lay down my life for them.

There is no greater love than this
that a man should lay down his life
for his friends
and you are my friends,
if you do what I have commanded.

Whoever believes in me,
I will never turn away.
Whoever has faith in me,
even though he or she dies,
will live forever.

Now I am going to my Father
and your Father,
to my God
and your God,
but I shall come back

and take you to myself,
that where I am, you may be also.

WE WILL LAY OUR BURDEN DOWN,
WE WILL LAY OUR BURDEN DOWN,
WE WILL LAY OUR BURDEN DOWN,
IN THE HANDS OF THE SON OF GOD.

⭘ Lord, where are you now?
Holy Week prayer 4

A prayer for Good Friday, which evokes the loss and seeming finality in the aftermath of Jesus' death.

Leader: So there it is,
the ugly shape of beautiful wood,
rough hewn by human hands.

ALL: LORD, WHERE ARE YOU NOW?

Leader: And there it is,
a tight-shut tomb,
a borrowed grave,
sealed with stone and silence.

ALL: LORD, WHERE ARE YOU NOW?

Leader: And there it is,
your broken body,
shrouded in linen,
clothed in darkness.

ALL: LORD, WHERE ARE YOU NOW?

Leader: And somewhere stand your people,
crying though tired of crying,
their eyes sore and bloodshot.
They will not sleep tonight.

ALL: LORD, WHERE ARE YOU NOW?

Leader: And out in the streets,
the children have stopped their playing,
the sound of music has gone sour,
even the unlikely people
fidget and wonder.

ALL: LORD, WHERE ARE YOU NOW?

Leader: And here are we,
saying,
"If only,"

murmuring,
"Surely not,"
counting the cost for once
of our carelessness
and our lovelessness
and our sin.

Trying so vainly to gain all,
we've bartered you away in the transaction.
We have lost the one who found us.

With the Peters and Marys of all time,
we wait,
for only you can tell
whether we are worth rising for.
AMEN.

When Jesus died
Holy Week meditation 4

The following meditation might be one of a variety of activities that take place on Good Friday (see page 125). It consists of a series of readings and prayers which were originally used on Good Friday evening on Iona. The focus is on the range of people who were left feeling desolate at Jesus' death, all of whom were present in different capacities at his end.

The meditation is basically designed in three sections, to be led by three people: a leader (who introduces prayer), a reader (who deals with scripture passages) and a cantor (who introduces the songs). There should be a minimal introduction.

A space other than a church is best to reflect that Jesus' followers would be in hiding, in private places. It should have a cross of small lit candles on a table in the center.

Suggested songs are shown below. These are all suitable for unaccompanied singing, and are either well known or traditional melodies. Others may be substituted. O SACRED HEAD, SORE WOUNDED and PRAISE TO THE HOLIEST IN THE HEIGHT can be found in most denominational hymnals; WHEN TROUBLE STRIKES (in the HEAVEN SHALL NOT WAIT collection), IF YOU BELIEVE AND I BELIEVE (in the SENT BY THE LORD collection).

Personnel: **Leader**
               Reader
               Cantor

Reader: *(May read Isaiah 53:1–9)*

(Song – O SACRED HEAD, SORE WOUNDED, verse 1 solo)

When Jesus died,
a number of women were present,
watching from a distance,
who had followed Jesus from Galilee

and looked after him.

Among them were Mary of Magdala,
Mary, the mother of James and Joseph,
the mother of the sons of Zebedee
and Salome.

These women had all followed him
as had many others
who had come up to Jerusalem with him.

There was also his own mother, Mary,
who had borne him and who watched him die.

Leader: And with them,
we might remember other women,
like Joanna, Martha, Susanna,
who had followed him,
      fed him
and tried to keep faithful to him
until the end.

Reader: He had always loved his own
who were in the world
and he loved them to the end.

Leader: Let us pray.

Let us, in kindness and gratitude,
remember and name before God,
women of today
who serve Jesus
or who long for his salvation.

(Silence during which names may be mentioned)

And let us remember and name
those women who, for whatever reason,
keep far from Christ.

(Silence during which names may be mentioned)

Reader: Jesus came into the world
not to condemn but to save.
May their eyes and our eyes
see that salvation.
AMEN.

(Song – WHEN TROUBLE STRIKES with verse 1 sung solo)

Reader: When Jesus died,
a number of men were present
besides the disciples who stood at a distance.

There was Simon of Cyrene,
who had been ordered to help carry Jesus' cross.
There was Nicodemus,
the man who had visited Jesus by night,
who came this time
with more than fifty pounds of myrrh and aloes
in order to embalm Jesus' body.

There was Joseph of Arimathea,
a wealthy man who,
when evening fell,
approached Pilate and asked for the body of Jesus.
He took it,
wrapped it in a clean linen sheet,
and laid it in an unused tomb
which had been cut out of the rock.
Then he rolled a large stone against the entrance.

Leader: And with them
we might remember other men,
like Zacchaeus, Lazarus, Levi,
who followed him,
    cared for him
and tried to keep faithful to him until the end.

Reader: He had always loved his own
who were in the world
and he loved them to the end.

Leader: Let us pray.

Let us, in kindness and gratitude,
remember and name before God
men of today,
who serve Jesus
or who long for his salvation.

(Silence during which names may be mentioned)

And let us remember and name

those men who, for whatever reason,
keep far from Christ.

(Silence during which names may be mentioned)

Reader: Jesus came into the world
not to condemn but to save.
May their eyes and our eyes
see that salvation.
AMEN.

*(Song – PRAISE TO THE HOLIEST IN THE HEIGHT,
verse 1 solo)*

Reader: When Jesus died,
a number of nations were present.

Pilate had an inscription written
and fastened to the cross.
It read, "Jesus of Nazareth, King of the Jews."
It was written in Hebrew, Latin and Greek.

And a Roman centurion was summoned by Pilate
to testify that Jesus was indeed dead.

Leader: And with these nations and peoples –
the Jews, the Greeks, the Romans –
we might remember others,
like the Samaritans,
for all of whom Jesus came,
in order that the world might be saved.

Reader: He had always loved his own
who were in the world
and he loved them to the end.

Leader: So let us remember and name before God
the nations and the peoples of today
for whom Jesus died
and pray for their peace.

(Silence during which names may be mentioned)

Reader: Jesus came into the world
not to condemn but to save.
May their eyes and our eyes
see that salvation.

AMEN.

(Song – IF YOU BELIEVE AND I BELIEVE, which the cantor should hum through once, then all sing three times)

Reader: We proclaim Christ nailed to the cross;
though this is an offense to some
and foolishness to others,
to those who are called,
no matter their status,
Christ is the power of God
and the wisdom of God.

So we declare ...

ALL: IN LIFE,
IN DEATH,
IN LIFE BEYOND DEATH,
JESUS CHRIST IS LORD.

↑ Holy Saturday
Holy Week symbolic action 7

Some churches have a full Easter Vigil with eucharist, lasting up to three hours. Where a congregation does not want to have such a lengthy vigil or to celebrate Holy Communion before Easter morning, the following pattern used in Iona Abbey might be adapted.

If it has not happened on Friday, and if the necessary material is available, it is very evocative to cover the places associated with God's grace with black cloth – the font, altar, pulpit, lectern or ambo, fixed crucifix or cross.

a) Gathering
People then assemble for a vigil late at night – say 11:30 pm. The church is dimly lit, people gather in silence and each is given an unlit candle.

b) Evocation of the past week
Up to fifteen minutes may be spent in recounting, through scripture or story, what happened from Palm Sunday until Holy Saturday with silences or a chant in between.

c) Lighting the church
When it comes towards midnight, the following words may be spoken leading to the speaker moving to the back of the church and bringing in a lighted candle from the vestibule.

A chant such as the IONA GLORIA or DEUS DE DEO (both from the COME ALL YOU PEOPLE collection) or an ALLELUIA (such as that by Norah Duncan from the THERE IS ONE AMONG US collection) is sung repeatedly, with people joining in the song only when they have lit their candle.

When almost the whole company is candlelit, the black cloths can be dramatically removed and any ornamentation previously taken out can be brought back in. The singing stops and an announcement of the resurrection, such as that shown on the next page, is made.

d) Celebration
One form of celebration, rarely used in church, is participative dance.
As it happens, the folk hymn LORD OF THE DANCE by Sydney Carter
is ideally suited to the movements of both THE GRAND OLD DUKE
OF YORK and the GAY GORDONS. On Iona, both have been done at
the same time, one in the choir area, the other in the south aisle.
Only those who want to join the dance, accompanied by appropriate
instruments. Others sing the song.

After a blessing, the assembly should recess singing an ALLELUIA
into the open air.

Leader: Just before daybreak,
Mary went to the tomb.

*(Here the large candle is lit from which others will
be lit)*

And a voice said, "Mary."

And a voice said,
"Why are you looking
for the living among the dead?
He is not here.
He is not here."

And a voice said,
"Don't be afraid.
But go and tell my friends
that they will see me."

*(Sung response – ALLELUIA, with each member of
the congregation standing and joining in as his/her
candle is lit)*

Leader: Praise the Lord for Christ is risen.
ALL: HE IS RISEN INDEED!

Leader: Sisters and brothers,
this is a great moment
when again we can declare,
that the love of God is stronger
than the sin of the world
and that nothing,

in the heights or depths
can separate us from God's love,
which is alive again in Christ Jesus.

The peace of the Lord Jesus Christ be with you.

ALL: AND ALSO WITH YOU.

I It was on the Saturday
Holy Week reading 9

This reading was originally printed as part of a larger piece consisting of the other IT WAS ON ... readings found in this book. It was primarily intended to be read by people on their own, as personal preparation for a series of workshops and reflections during Holy Week.

Alternatively, it may be read in a similar way, but on its own on the Saturday of Holy Week.

It was on the Saturday
that he was not there.

Those who don't like corpses
can't stay away from graveyards,
unless there's some prohibition to stop them
revisiting the dead end
of their hopes and their dreams.

It's as if they think
that should the voice speak again,
it will speak there
or a sunbeam will dance
or a flower will shoot
and give a sign of misinterpreted life.

But close the cemetery,
or confine, through custom or constraint,
the wailing ones to the house
and it looms larger ...
the loss,
the lostness,
the losers.

Men shiver in an upstairs room,
warm though the day is.
Women weep in an uncharmed circle.

Memory is forced on memory.
The mind's eye tries to trace
the profile and the face,
the smile,
the gentle twitching of the nose ...
and fails.
And a panic sets in
because it seems he can't be remembered.
Was he ever known?

It was on the Saturday
that he was not there.

We need you, God
Holy Week reading 10

This is the text for a song of the same name which can be adequately read as a poem on the evening prior to Easter Day. The music can be found in the ENEMY OF APATHY collection.

We fear you, God:
you dare to come
offending from the virgin womb.
Through this and through the suckling breast,
our sense of decency you test
'til worldly life is weaned and blessed.

We fear you, God:
you dare enjoy
the clothes and accents we employ.
Through these and through the folk you meet,
eternity on earth you greet
and shock pretentious faith's elite.

We fear you, God:
you dare arrive
powerless and poor where tyrants thrive.
Through this and through the naked cross,
security is charged with loss
as love on hatred you emboss.

We need you, God,
for you come near
to where we are and what we fear.
Our raw humanity you wear,
our limits to the tomb you bear
'til these, redeemed by love, you share.

When finest aspirations fail
Holy Week reading 11

These words of a song to be sung after the remembrance of the cruci-fixion, perhaps on Holy Saturday, can equally well be read as a poem. It aims to associate all the brokenness which we experience with the brokenness of Christ, in order that, through him and in imitation of him, disintegrated lives may be made new. The music to which the words are set can be found in the COURAGE TO SAY NO collection.

When finest aspirations fail
and dreams become dismay,
and all the hopes tomorrow held
lie felled by yesterday,
what can we do, where do we turn,
what can we say?

We hurt for what has happened
and we fear for what's to come;
and easy consolation leaves us
negative and numb,
and wondering whether deeper depths
are yet to plumb.

Shall they control our destiny
who, deaf to our demands,
are ruled by other values
and defer to their commands?
And are our futures safe
in these unwanted hands?

Oh, Christ, you lost control,
or so it seems, when to a tree
they nailed you and regaled you
and refused to set you free;
and all because you showed
how life was meant to be.

Then must our hopes, like you,
be broken down beyond repair;
must we be lost and powerless,
befriended by despair,
in order somehow to be saved
and sense God's care?

And shall our hopes, like you,
arise from where they ceased to be;
and shall the spirit that was crushed
be transformed and set free?
If that's God's will, then we await
what's yet to be.

△ This is the Good News
Easter affirmation 1

A set of responses to announce the Resurrection, after which the Peace may be shared.

Leader: This is the Good News –
the grave is empty,
Christ is risen.

ALL: HALLELUJAH!

Leader: This is the Good News –
the light shines in the darkness
and the darkness can never put it out.

ALL: HALLELUJAH!

Leader: This is the Good News –
once we were no people,
now we are God's people.

ALL: HALLELUJAH!

Leader: Christ is our peace,
the indestructible peace
we now share with each other.

Lord God, early in the morning
Easter prayer 1

Leader: Lord God,
early in the morning,
when the world was young,
you made life in all its beauty and terror;
you gave birth to all that we know.

Hallowed be your name,
ALL: HALLOWED BE YOUR NAME.

Leader: Early in the morning,
when the world least expected it,
a newborn child crying in a cradle
announced that you had come among us,
that you were one of us.

Hallowed be your name,
ALL: HALLOWED BE YOUR NAME.

Leader: Early in the morning,
surrounded by respectable liars,
religious leaders,
anxious statesmen
and silent friends,
you accepted the penalty for doing good,
for being God:
you shouldered and suffered the cross.

Hallowed be your name,
ALL: HALLOWED BE YOUR NAME.

Leader: Early in the morning,
a voice in a guarded graveyard
and footsteps in the dew
proved that you had risen,
that you had come back
to those and for those
who had forgotten, denied and destroyed you.

Hallowed be your name,
ALL: HALLOWED BE YOUR NAME.

Leader: This morning,
in the multi-colored company
of your Church on earth and in heaven,
we celebrate your creation, your life,
your death and resurrection,
your interest in us;
so we pray,

ALL: LORD, BRING NEW LIFE,
WHERE WE ARE WORN AND TIRED;
NEW LOVE,
WHERE WE HAVE TURNED HARD-HEARTED;
FORGIVENESS,
WHERE WE FEEL HURT
AND WHERE WE HAVE WOUNDED;
AND THE JOY AND FREEDOM
OF YOUR HOLY SPIRIT,
WHERE WE ARE PRISONERS OF OURSELVES.

(A silence)

Leader: To all and to each,
on his community and on his friends,
where regret is real,
Jesus pronounces his pardon
and grants us the right to begin again.
Thanks be to God!

ALL: AMEN.

△ How excellent the name
Easter litany 1

This litany focuses on the many symbolic allusions to planting, growing and harvesting in the life and sayings of Jesus. If desired, the recurring words of the response can be replaced by a sung response, such as JESUS CHRIST, JESUS CHRIST from the THERE IS ONE AMONG US collection.

Leader: Christ,
Christ, the branch,
the shoot from the tree of David,
Christ, the gardener,
the pruner,
the one who cuts back in kindness,

Cantor: O Lord, in all the earth,
ALL: O LORD, IN ALL THE EARTH,
Leader: how excellent the name,
ALL: HOW EXCELLENT THE NAME OF JESUS.

Leader: Christ,
Christ, the leaf
the tender shoot in dry ground,
Christ, the nature lover,
the flower admirer,
the one who expects us to be attractive for him,

Cantor: O Lord, in all the earth,
ALL: O LORD, IN ALL THE EARTH,
Leader: how excellent the name,
ALL: HOW EXCELLENT THE NAME OF JESUS.

Leader: Christ,
Christ, the seed,
the corn gatherer,
Christ, the germ of resurrection,
the first fruit of heaven,
the one who makes us and all things new,

Cantor:	O Lord, in all the earth,
ALL:	O LORD, IN ALL THE EARTH,
Leader:	how excellent the name,
ALL:	HOW EXCELLENT THE NAME OF JESUS.

Leader:	Jesus Christ,
	branch and leaf and seed,
	from whom we come,
	with whom we stay,
	to whom we return,
ALL:	YOU WE BLESS,
	NAME ABOVE ALL NAMES,
	AND EXCELLENT IN ALL THE EARTH.
	AMEN.

Jesus Christ, we greet you!
Easter prayer 2

The first sign Jesus made to reveal his resurrection to Mary was to speak her name. Echoing that encounter, this prayer is particularly appropriate for early Easter Day.

Leader: Jesus Christ, we greet you!
Your hands still have holes in them,
your feet are wet from the dew;
and with the memory of our names
undimmed by three days of death
you meet us,
risen from the grave.

We fail to understand how;
we puzzle at the reason why.

But you have come:
not to answer our questions,
but to show us your face.

ALL: YOU ARE ALIVE
AND THE WORLD CAN REJOICE AGAIN.
HALLELUJAH!
AMEN

Tom in two

Easter reading 1

This poem celebrates how the resurrection hallows the whole of life. It can also be sung to the English traditional folk melody THE SUSSEX CAROL.

When sight and insight lose their way,
we segregate familiar ground
from where we think you ought to stay
and peace and paradise abound:
in Christ you tore the barrier down –
the Word made flesh let heaven be known.

When Holy Grace took human form
and called earth's outcast people his friends,
when Heaven's Original revealed
the path required to make amends.
We felt compelled to fret and fuss.
You know – for you were there with us.

In warm embrace for withered arms,
in dining out with tarnished guests,
in breaking umpleen petty rules,
in controversial, quiet requests,
barriers dividing heaven from earth
were bulldozed to reveal our worth.

Still, we are reticent to see
that all of life is yours to save,
that peace and poverty and power
adorn your birthplace and your grave,
that, rising, you redeemed the fraud
of virtue trying to shelter God.

Ah, Holy Jesus, come again
wherever we would keep you out.
Destroy our sanctimonious shrouds
to demonstrate, to all who doubt,
the Temple's veil is torn in two
and all of life is sacred now.

I It was on the Sunday (ii)
Easter reading 2

This reading was originally printed as part of a larger piece consisting of the other IT WAS ON ... readings found in this book. It was primarily intended to be read by people on their own, as personal preparation for a series of workshops and reflections during Holy Week.

Alternatively, it may be read in a similar way, but on its own on Easter Day.

It was on the Sunday
that he pulled the corn.

They arrived with flowers,
shuffling through the dawn
as the dawn snuffed out
the last candles of night.
Their faces betrayed their belief
that yesterday would always be better
than tomorrow,
despite what he said.
He would not say it again,
so why bother to believe him on that score?

And the flowers,
they too were silent witnesses to disbelief.
Like the grass,
they were cut to be dried to death,
cut off from the root,
the bulb, the source of life.
He was the flower they cherished,
the flower now perished
whose fate the lilies of the field,
now tight in hand,
would re-enact.

So when they passed the crouched figure
at the edge of the road,

they thought little of him,
scarcely seeing his form through their tears.
Had they looked even a little,
they would have seen a man
letting grain fall through his fingers,
dropping to the earth
to die and yet to rise again.
It was on the Sunday
that he pulled the corn.

The three women
Easter script 1

Each of the three female readers should preferably read from a lectern or similar position (pulpit, table/altar), where the script has already been placed. In this way, their hands will be free to carry flowers. They should read almost on top of each other, as if both excited and disappointed. When both entering and exiting they might move quickly, if not quite running.

Personnel: **A**
              B
              C

A: We went there ...

B: first thing ...

C: the three of us.

A: It was very damp ...

B: there was a heavy dew ...

C: you could see the sun rising.

A: We took some flowers ...

B: I picked them on Friday ...

C: and we took some perfume ...

A: we thought there would be a smell ...

B: you know the way corpses go ...

C: I was scared.

A: It was just us ...

B: the men wouldn't come ...

C: they were scared like me.

A: We ran up the road ...

B: we were out of breath ...

C: but we walked through the graveyard.

A: We wondered about the stone ...

B: who would roll it away?

C: We should have brought the men.

A: And then we looked ...

B & C: THE STONE WAS AWAY!

A: I went in first.

B: I was terrified.

C: I never wanted to go.

A: There was nothing there ...

B: there were just bandages ...

C: right where we had left him.

A: But no body ...

B: and then we heard a voice...

C: but it wasn't his voice.

A: It said he was risen.

B: It said he wasn't there.

C: It said we had to tell the others.

A: So we've to go back ...

B: but who will believe us?

C: They'll think we're mad.

A: We've to tell the others ...

B: but they'll never believe us ...

C: they'll say that we're just stupid women.

A: But the stone was rolled away ...

B: and the body wasn't there ...

C: and we did hear a voice ...

A, B & C: AND HE IS RISEN!

Glory be to you

Easter prayer 3

Leader: Glory be to you,
ALL: GOD, OUR STRENGTH AND OUR REDEEMER.

Leader: The vacant cross and the empty tomb
vindicate your claim
that the love which suffers
is the love which saves.

So fill your people with joy
and your Church with celebration
ALL: THAT THE WORLD MAY KNOW
THAT YOUR HOLY SON JESUS
IS NOT A DEAD HERO WE COMMEMORATE,
BUT THE LIVING LORD WE WORSHIP,
TO WHOM, WITH YOU AND THE HOLY SPIRIT,
BE OUR PRAISE FOREVER.
AMEN.

↑ Christ has died, Christ is risen
Easter symbolic action 1

During the litany, the congregation may participate in two possible ways. The first is for people to say aloud the name of any saint or martyr of the Church, well or lesser known, whom they wish to remember. The second is by planting a seed in a large bowl as a sign of their desire to be part of the kingdom's work.

This may be done in silence or preferably as instrumental music is played or a response, such as the Honduran ALLELUIA (from the COME ALL YOU PEOPLE collection) or MAYENZIWE (from the MANY & GREAT collection), is sung. To enable this, a table should be positioned centrally, easily accessible to the congregation. On it a cross should be placed, in front of which there should be a large bowl or tray containing earth, and at least one smaller bowl containing seeds.

(All standing)

Leader: Eternal God,
your Word declares
that the love which is laid down in faith
will be raised and produce a great harvest.
This we celebrate as we proclaim:

ALL: CHRIST HAS DIED,
CHRIST IS RISEN,
CHRIST WILL COME AGAIN.

Leader: We remember and praise you
for the saints and martyrs of this and every age.
We name them before you now.

(Remaining where they are standing, people are invited to name saints and martyrs.)

Leader: These lives, like seeds, dropped to the ground;
yet their witness has borne fruit
and enables us to say:

ALL: CHRIST HAS DIED,
CHRIST IS RISEN,
CHRIST WILL COME AGAIN.

Leader: We pray for your Church throughout the world
and for that part to which we belong,
that it may be ready to spend
and to be spent in your service,
that the love of self-preservation
may be set aside,
that the deaths you demand of it
may be embraced joyfully,
and that through all it may proclaim:

ALL: CHRIST HAS DIED,
CHRIST IS RISEN,
CHRIST WILL COME AGAIN.

Leader: In silence,
we surrender ourselves
and all that we count important
to your will and purpose.

For we cannot know
the glory of Christ's resurrection
if we do not have the fellowship of his sufferings.

And we cannot expect to gather the kingdom's
harvest
if we do not sow the kingdom's seed.

*(People are invited to plant their seed in the large
bowl or tray as the chant is sung continuously)*

Leader: In us and through us,
may your Spirit proclaim:

ALL: CHRIST HAS DIED,
CHRIST IS RISEN,
CHRIST WILL COME AGAIN.

Here are your disciples
Easter prayer 4

Leader: Lord Jesus,
here are your disciples –
your wounded hands and feet
in the world today are ours.

At times we have been the frightened ones,
staying at a distance,
worried about our safety or our reputations.
But you come close to us,
bringing peace and challenge,
unlocking our potential
and setting us free.

At times we have been the doubting ones,
when creeds conflict
or certainty has evaded us.
But you come close
and allow us to speak our minds,
accepting us
and setting us free.

At times we have been the confused ones,
feeling far from you
with questions that don't have answers.
So, in the evening of your resurrection
we listen for your voice.

(Silence)

The risen Christ says to us:
"Peace be with you.
As the Father sent me,
so I am sending you."

As the body of Christ,
let us join hands.

(ALL join hands)

ALL: THROUGH OUR FEAR,
THROUGH OUR DOUBT,
THROUGH OUR CONFUSION
MAY WE CONTINUE JESUS' WORK
AS WE TRAVEL MANY ROADS,
LIBERATED AND UNITED
BY THE LOVE OF THE RESURRECTED ONE.
AMEN.

Easter evening
Easter reading 3

A reading for the evening of Easter Day. The poem describes the two disciples' journey from confusion and sorrow to recognition and joy as they encounter Jesus on the Emmaus road. The text is that of a song which can be found in THE LAST JOURNEY collection, set to the traditional Scottish melody THE SILKIE.

As we walked home at close of day,
a stranger joined us on our way.
He heard us speak of one who'd gone
and when we stopped, he carried on.

"Why wander further without light?
Please stay with us this troubled night.
We've shared the truth of how we feel
and now would like to share a meal."

We sat to eat our simple spread,
then watched the stranger take the bread;
and, as he said the blessing prayer,
we knew that someone else was there.

No stranger he; it was our eyes
which failed to see, in stranger's guise,
the Lord who, risen from the dead,
met us when ready to be fed.

Alleluia! Alleluia!
Alleluia! Alleluia!
As Mary and our sisters said,
the Lord is risen from the dead!

Jesus Christ, you meet us

Easter prayer 5

A prayer suitable for use on the evening of Easter Day, particularly following a reading or presentation of the Emmaus road story.

_____

Leader: Jesus Christ, you meet us;
your hands still holed,
but your breath warm,
and your conversation engaging.
Death has not changed your accent
or diminished your love.

And though the world
should still show signs of its imperfection,
the good news is that you have destined it
and all its people to be made whole.

ALL: SO, AS ON THIS EASTER EVENING
WE ARE GATHERED IN YOUR HOUSE
AND CHEERED BY YOUR GOSPEL,
JOIN US,
AS YOU JOINED YOUR FIRST DISCIPLES
AND MAKE OUR WORSHIP YOUR EMMAUS ROAD.
AMEN.

△ In life, in death
Easter responses 1

Leader: In life, in death,
in life beyond death,
ALL: JESUS CHRIST IS LORD.

Leader: Over powers and principalities,
over all who determine, control,
govern or finance the affairs of humankind,
ALL: JESUS CHRIST IS LORD.

Leader: Of the poor, of the broken,
of the sinned against and the sinner,
ALL: JESUS CHRIST IS LORD.

Leader: Above the Church,
beyond our most excellent theologies
and in the quiet corners of our hearts,
ALL: JESUS CHRIST IS LORD.

Leader: Thanks be to God.
ALL: AMEN.

Resurrection remembrances (i)
Easter meditation 1

Here are four testimonies of people who, for different reasons, did not expect to meet the resurrected Jesus. These may be used on their own or followed by RESURRECTION REMEMBRANCES (ii), page 205, which is a prayer with symbolic action.

Between each reflection, a short song or chant is sung, such as the reflective Honduran ALLELUIA (from the COME ALL YOU PEOPLE collection). During the singing, a symbol representing each set of disciples is placed at a different "station" or table (identified by a large lit candle) at different points in the church. Readers A, B and C may stand at these points with D speaking from a central position.

The symbols might be as follows: A (the ones who were afraid), a key; B (the ones who were confused), bread; C (the one who doubted), wood and nails.

Personnel: **A,** *a disciple*
B, *Cleopas*
C, *Thomas*
D, *a disciple*

A:
We had not been expecting him ...
and yet we had.

We were frightened,
because he had been killed
and they might be looking for us.

Then, when some of the women said
that they had seen him,
we were more frightened than ever.

We had denied him,
abandoned him,
watched him die at a distance,
and kept quiet about our previous
association.

What would he do with us now?

We sat, huddled in an upstairs room,
locked away from the world,
afraid of "them,"
afraid of him,
sitting silently
with the shades down.

But he came
and unlocked every door
with his unexpected words,
"Peace ...
Peace be with you.

I am sending you ... out."

B: There were two of us,
walking together,
walking away from it all;

walking and talking,
no ... more than talking...
arguing,
arguing and almost falling out.

We agreed on what had happened,
we knew what had happened,
we were there.

But what did it mean?

The kind of revolution we wanted
was not what we were given.

And if he had set Israel free,
why was he not around
to proclaim its liberation?

So, it was good
to have the company of a stranger,
who was as interested in current affairs as
     ourselves.
It was good to have somebody
make sense of our confusion,
draw together the loose threads we had forgotten.

Though it wasn't until we sat down
to share a meal
that our confusion really ended,
when his feeding of us began.

C: For a week I heard the same story
from each of them,
and the more often I heard it,
the less I believed it.

We had all been through a lot.
We were in a mess.
The unthinkable had happened,
and we were lost,
                guilty
                and grieving.

I thought that maybe the death hadn't sunk in;
I thought they were refusing to come to terms with
  it,
pretending that it hadn't happened.

His hands had touched us,
his breath had blessed us,
but now they were cold
and he was gone
and all that was left was memory.

Yet, in all my doubt,
I envied them,
until doubt vanished
and faith kindled again
when a well-known voice said,
"Put your hands here."

D: We don't see much of him now,
though we've met several times.

He's touched us,
talked to us,
and even cooked breakfast for us
on an open fire.

But he's going soon.

He's said as much,

though how and when
we'll not know until it happens.
And though we don't want it that way,
we know that he has to go ...
so that his work can finish
and ours can begin.

↑ Resurrection remembrances (ii)
Easter symbolic action 2

This prayer and symbolic action is intended to be used in conjunction with the previous meditation.

There should be three "stations" or tables around the church, each with a symbol representing the stories reflected on in RESURRECTION REMEMBRANCES (i), page 201, and beside each there should be a large lit candle.

During the sung response SEND OUT YOUR LIGHT (from the COME ALL YOU PEOPLE collection) people are invited to light a small votive candle for themselves or someone brought to mind by these reflections, placing it at the appropriate station.

After all who wish to do so have lit their candles, prayers are said at each station before people return to their seats. The prayers of A, B and C may be spoken at the same time as each other, since each is specific to those standing around that particular "station." D's prayer would then follow. Alternatively, all four prayers may be spoken one after the other so that all may hear them. This is also more appropriate for places of worship where space is limited and where there is not enough room for people to remain standing around the three "stations."

The responses DO YOU LOVE ME? on page 212 may be read immediately after the symbolic action, while people are still standing at the stations; and this in turn may be followed by the song YOU HEAR THE LAMBS A-CRYIN' (from the COURAGE TO SAY NO collection) during which people return to their seats.

It may be felt necessary also to include some of the detail above in the leader's opening invitation as well as on the service sheet/order of worship, for the sake of clarity.

Personnel: **Leader**
                   A, *the ones who were afraid*
                   B, *the ones who were confused*
                   C, *the ones who doubted*
                   D

Leader: For some people, actions speak louder than words,
so in this prayer we may,
if we wish,
make a sign of our intentions.

There are three stations around the church,
each with a symbol
representing the stories we've just reflected on:
a key ... for those who were afraid;
bread ... for those who were confused;
wood and nails ... for the one who doubted.

If, for whatever reason,
we wish to meet Jesus in an area of our lives
where there is fear, confusion or doubt,
we may move,
when the chant begins,
to the appropriate place and light a small candle
which represents the light of Christ,
and set it down beside the symbol.

If, alternatively,
we have someone in mind
who is consumed by fear, confusion or doubt,
we may light a candle
to accompany our prayer for them.

After lighting your candle,
please step back,
but stay standing around the station,
as short prayers will be said at each place.

*(The sung response is sung continuously, as people
move to light a candle. Once all who wish to have
done so, the following prayers are spoken.)*

A: Lord Jesus,
here are your disciples
and those we represent
who need to meet you in the midst of fear.

Travel the distance we have traveled from you,
dispel our anxieties about ourselves,
our past, our faith,
and open from the outside
the hearts we unlock to you from within.

B: Lord Jesus,
here are your disciples
and those we represent
who need to meet you in the midst of confusion.

Help us to identify your voice
beneath and above all the other voices we hear,
convince us that there is a calm
at the heart of the storm;
and feed our faith
on the certainty of your presence
and all your promises.

C: Lord Jesus,
here are your disciples
and those we represent
who need to meet you in our doubt.

Help us to hold graciously
those questions to which there are no easy
   answers,
enable us to discern the inability to believe
which comes from our unwillingness to obey,
and in the pain and scarring of the world,
help us to identify your hands,
wounded among us.

D: Lord Jesus,
glorious and resurrected,
and willing the best for us
and daring us to smile with you
as we walk behind you,
give us your hopefulness,
give us your toughness,
give us your peace.
AMEN.

Thomas reflecting
Easter script 2

This script should be read in a reflective manner, as if the words are being pondered as they are spoken for the first time by Thomas. If desired, one verse of the song HOW LONG, O LORD (from the WHEN GRIEF IS RAW collection) may be used at the appropriate point. The Scottish word "thole" may be replaced by its English equivalent, "stand."

Thomas: I expected him to scold me,
not – as you might think –
for doubting.

We had all doubted, at different times,
and he was never angry.

Indeed, he doubted himself, sometimes,
or if he didn't,
he certainly understood how it felt,
because he would sing the Psalms of doubt
with great fervor.

(Sung response)

Doubt wasn't an enemy to him.
He could stand us doubting.
It was indifference he couldn't stand:
indifference and apathy.

(Pause)

I expected him to scold me
perhaps for making conditions.

I did do that and I won't deny it.

"If only I see this and do that ... then I'll believe."

What a fool,

thinking I could make conditions with God,
but he didn't take me to task.

He saw that I was happy because I had seen
and he said that they were also happy
who believed without making conditions,
without saying "if only" or "unless."

(Pause)

I expected him to scold me
because I wasn't there when he came.

The others were present, I was absent.
It wasn't their fault or his fault.
It was mine.
I had – for whatever reason –
decided that it was all finished.

He came back to say it was all beginning.

(Pause)

I expected him to scold me.
But he didn't.
He gave me his hand
and, more than that,
he gave me his peace.

Peter's testimony
Easter script 3

Here Peter recalls the meeting with Jesus on the lakeshore, as told in John 21:1–19.

Peter: There was nothing else to do,
so I went back to fishing.

We knew he was alive;
we had seen him
and then he went away
without leaving instructions.

So I said, "Let's go back to the fishing,"
and the others agreed.
I mean, we had to feed ourselves somehow.
You can't just exist on fresh air and memories.

So we went back to the fishing
and caught nothing.
I wondered if we had lost our touch
or if ... and I hesitate to say this ...
it was some kind of punishment from God.

And then, in the morning,
somebody shouted that our nets were on the
  wrong side.
"What does he know?" I grunted,
but to please the others, I hauled them in
and then cast them back out.

And when the net began to strain,
I had this funny feeling in the pit of my stomach.
"What does he know?" I had grunted.
Now I knew who "he" was,
and knew that he knew everything.

When we got back to the shore,
he didn't give me or any of us a scolding,

he just said,
"Would you like some breakfast?"
And then he fed us
so that ...

I only realized why he had fed us
when, in a private moment,
he looked me straight in the face three times
and said,
"Do you love me, Peter?"

The first time I was embarrassed;
the second time I was annoyed;
the third time I was convinced.

"Yes, I love you ... you know I do!"

Then feed my lambs
and feed my lambs
and feed my sheep.

And then I realized that he had fed us,
so that we could feed others;
and that he loved us,
so that we could love others the same way.

Do you love me?
Easter affirmation 2

*This simple scripted reading, which may be used following RESUR-
RECTION REMEMBRANCES (ii) on page 205, may be used as an act
of commitment. Peter's responses to Jesus' questions should be read
by the entire congregation and, ideally, all should be standing. The
poignant song YOU HEAR THE LAMBS A-CRYIN' (from the COUR-
AGE TO SAY NO collection) could very appropriately follow.*

Personnel: **Narrator**
Jesus
Peter

Narrator: The third time Jesus appeared to the disciples
after he was raised from death,
he said to Simon Peter:

Jesus: Simon, son of John,
do you love me more than all else?

PETER: YES, LORD, YOU KNOW THAT I LOVE YOU.

Jesus: Take care of my lambs.

Simon, son of John, do you love me?

PETER: YES, LORD, YOU KNOW THAT I LOVE YOU.

Jesus: Take care of my sheep.

Simon, son of John, do you love me?

PETER: LORD, YOU KNOW EVERYTHING,
YOU KNOW THAT I LOVE YOU!

Jesus: Take care of my sheep.

Through the rising of your Son
Easter prayer 6

Leader: Almighty God,
through the rising of your Son from the grave,
you broke the power of the grave,
you broke the power of death
and condemned death itself to die.

As we celebrate this great triumph
may we also make it the model for our living.

ALL: HELP US TO IDENTIFY IN OUR LIVES
ALL THAT SHOULD RIGHTLY DIE –
REDUNDANT RELATIONSHIPS,
TIRED HABITS,
FRUITLESS LONGINGS.

RESURRECT IN OUR LIVES
FAITH, HOPE AND LOVE
AS SURELY AS YOU RAISED JESUS CHRIST
FROM THE GRAVE.
AMEN.

The Savior leaves
Easter reading 4

This is the text of a song of the same name which can adequately be read as a poem and which deals with Jesus' ascension. The music it is set to can be found in the ENEMY OF APATHY collection.

Forsaking chariots of fire
and fanfared brass,
as strangely silent as he came,
the Savior leaves
and God, with heaven's caress,
the Son receives.

He has to go, as from the grave
he had to rise:
in order to be everywhere
he must depart
to live, not in one place,
but in each heart.

So, Christ ascends; air cradles him,
disciples stare.
Their Easter joy, his seven weeks' stay
seem now to end.
But no! The Spirit's sending
they portend.

Let angel harmonies resound;
let trumpets blare;
let heaven's banquet guests applaud
the welcomed Word,
and earth anticipate
her coming Lord.

Blessing and honor
Easter prayer 7

A prayer suitable for Ascension Sunday.

Leader: Blessing and honor and glory and power!

Our words echo the praise of the angels
as you, Jesus Christ,
rise above the limitations of earth,
to sit forever on the right hand side of God.

No longer restricted to one place,
you are seated on the throne of heaven
and present in all places.

ALL: WE PRAISE YOU,
OUR GLORIOUS LORD AND SAVIOR
AND ARE FOREVER GLAD
THAT NOW THERE IS IN HEAVEN
ONE WHO UNDERSTANDS AND INTERCEDES
FOR US.

Leader: Though now we cannot ascend
to where you are,
still raise our hopes and hearts.

ALL: SO MAY OUR DISCIPLESHIP IN THIS WORLD
BE TOUCHED WITH THE GLORY OF HEAVEN
AND OUR LIVES BE SIGNS AND PROMISES
OF THE FULLNESS OF THE LIFE TO COME.
AMEN.

△ Today and tomorrow
Easter responses 2

Leader: Today and tomorrow,
ALL: TODAY AND TOMORROW,

Leader: Lo, I am with you always,
ALL: WHEN WE TRY
TO DO YOUR WILL,

Leader: I am with you always,
ALL: WHEN WE GO
WHERE WE DO NOT KNOW,

Leader: I am with you always,
ALL: WHEN WE MEET
ONE WE DO NOT RECOGNIZE,

Leader: I am with you always,
ALL: WHERE FAITH ENDS
AND DOUBT BEGINS,

Leader: I am with you always.
ALL: AND SHOULD WE FORGET YOU ...

Leader: I am with you always.
ALL: TODAY AND TOMORROW,
TODAY AND TOMORROW,
YOU ARE WITH US ALWAYS
TO THE END OF THE WORLD.
AMEN.

Sources of suggested chants and sung responses

A woman's care John L. Bell & Graham Maule;
Heaven shall not wait (GIA Publications, Inc.) G-3646
When grief is raw (GIA Publications, Inc.) G-4829
Alleluia Honduran traditional;
Come all you people (GIA Publications, Inc.) G-4391
Alleluia Norah Duncan IV;
There is one among us (GIA Publications, Inc) G-5111
Behold the Lamb of God John L. Bell;
Come all you people GIA Publications, Inc.) G-4391
Bless the Lord, my soul Taizé Community;
Songs and prayers from Taizé (Geoffrey Chapman/
Mowbray)
Songs of God's people (Oxford University Press)
Deus de Deo John L. Bell;
Come all you people (GIA Publications, Inc.) G-4391
Easter evening John L. Bell & Graham Maule;
Enemy of apathy (GIA Publications, Inc.) G-3647
Hallelujah Abraham Maraire;
Songs of God's people (Oxford University Press)
Have mercy on us *(Khudaya, Rahem Kar)* R.F. Liberius;
Love & anger (GIA Publications, Inc.) G-4947
How long, O Lord John L. Bell & Graham Maule
Heaven shall not wait (GIA Publications, Inc.) G-3646
When grief is raw (GIA Publications, Inc.) G-4829
I will give what I have John L. Bell & Graham Maule;
Enemy of apathy (GIA Publications, Inc.) G-3647
If you believe and I believe Zimbabwean traditional;
Sent by the Lord (GIA Publications, Inc.) G-3740
Iona Gloria traditional
Come all you people (GIA Publications, Inc.) G-4391
Jesus Christ, Son of God among us John L. Bell;
There is one among us (GIA Publications, Inc.) G-5111
Jesus Christ, Lover of all John L. Bell & Graham Maule
Heaven shall not wait (GIA Publications, Inc.) G-3646
Kyrie eleison (various) John L. Bell
Enemy of apathy (GIA Publications, Inc.) G-3647
Love from below (GIA Publications, Inc.) G-3648
Come all you people (GIA Publications, Inc.) G-4391
There is one among us (GIA Publications, Inc.) G-5111

Kyrie eleison Russian Orthodox;
>> Many & great (GIA Publications, Inc.) G-3649
>> Songs of God's people (Oxford University Press)

Kyrie eleison Taizé Community;
>> Songs and prayers from Taizé (Geoffrey Chapman/ Mowbray)

Lord of the dance Sydney Carter;
>> Songs of God's people (Oxford University Press)

Miserere nobis John L. Bell
>> Love from below (GIA Publications, Inc.) G-3648

O Lord, hear my prayer Taizé Community;
>> Songs and prayers from Taizé (Geoffrey Chapman/ Mowbray)
>> Songs of God's people (Oxford University Press)

Oh where are you going? John L. Bell & Graham Maule
>> Heaven shall not wait (GIA Publications, Inc.) G-3646

Ride on, ride on John L. Bell & Graham Maule
>> Enemy of apathy (GIA Publications, Inc.) G-3647

Send out your light John L. Bell
>> Come all you people (GIA Publications, Inc.) G-4391

Take, O take me as I am John L. Bell
>> Come all you people (GIA Publications, Inc.) G-4391

The Saviour leaves John L. Bell & Graham Maule
>> Enemy of apathy (GIA Publications, Inc.) G-3647

The servant John L. Bell & Graham Maule
>> Enemy of apathy (GIA Publications, Inc.) G-3647

Torn in two John L. Bell & Graham Maule;
>> Enemy of apathy (GIA Publications, Inc.) G-3647

We need you, God John L. Bell & Graham Maule
>> Enemy of apathy (GIA Publications, Inc.) G-3647

We will lay our burden down John L. Bell & Graham Maule
>> Love from below (GIA Publications, Inc.) G-3648

When finest aspirations fail John L. Bell
>> The courage to say no (GIA Publications, Inc.) G-4244

Wonder and stare John L. Bell
>> Enemy of apathy (GIA Publications, Inc.) G-3647
>> Come all you people (GIA Publications, Inc.) G-4391

You hear the lambs a-cryin' African American spiritual;
>> The courage to say no (GIA Publications, Inc.) G-4244

Major Feasts of the Seasons with their themes

SEASON OF LENT

Ash Wednesday   Penitence and fasting.

Lent 1   Temptation.

Lent 2   Jesus foretells his end.

Lent 3   Change your ways.

Lent 4   Jesus as light and restorer.

Lent 5   Delivery from death.

Lent 6   Passion/ Palm Sunday.
The ride into Jerusalem (most churches)
Overview of the Passion narratives
        (Roman Catholic church)

HOLY WEEK

Monday   The cleansing of the Temple

Tuesday   The dispute with the Pharisees.
The cursing of the tree.

Wednesday   The woman at the table, preparing Christ for burial.

Thursday   Judas.
The Last Supper.
Betrayal and arrest.

Friday   The denials.
The trials.
Scourging.
The Way of the Cross.
Crucifixion.
Burial.

Saturday	Silence.
	Waiting.

EASTER

Easter 1	Resurrection.
	The role of women.
	The Emmaus road.
Easter 2	Thomas and doubting.
Easter 3	Jesus appears to the disciples.
Easter 4	Jesus foretells his departure.
Easter 5	The promise of the Holy Spirit.
Ascension	Jesus returns to heaven.
Easter 6	The gift of peace.
Easter 7	Jesus' prayer to God for his disciples.

Readings for the Seasons

The regular readings are taken from the three-year Lectionary which, for the greater part, is shared by Roman Catholic, Anglican and Protestant churches.

YEAR A
Beginning on the First Sunday of Advent in 1998, 2001, 2004, 2007, 2010, 2013, 2016

YEAR B
Beginning on the First Sunday of Advent in 1999, 2002, 2005, 2008, 2011, 2014, 2017

YEAR C
Beginning on the First Sunday of Advent in 2000, 2003, 2006, 2009, 2012, 2015, 2018

SEASON OF LENT

Ash Wednesday

	YEAR A	YEAR B	YEAR C
Joel	2 : 1 - 2, 12 - 17	2 : 1 - 2, 12 - 17	2 : 1 - 2, 12 - 17
or Isaiah	58 : 1 - 12	58 : 1 - 12	58 : 1 - 12
Psalm	51 : 1 - 17	51 : 1 - 17	51 : 1 - 17
2 Corinthians	5 : 20b- 6:10	5 : 20b- 6:10	5 : 20b- 6:10
St. Matthew	6 : 1 - 6, 16 - 21	6 : 1 - 6, 16 - 21	6 : 1 - 6, 16 - 21

First Sunday in Lent

	YEAR A	YEAR B	YEAR C
Genesis (A) / Genesis (B) / Deuteronomy (C)	2 : 15 - 17 / 3 : 1 - 7	9 : 8 - 17	26 : 1 - 11
Psalm	32	25 : 1 - 10	91 : 1 - 2, 9 - 16
Romans (A) / 1 Peter (B) / Romans (C)	5 : 12 - 19	3 : 18 - 22	10 : 8b - 13
St. Matthew (A) / St. Mark (B) / St. Luke (C)	4 : 1 - 11	1 : 9 - 15	4 : 1 - 13

Second Sunday in Lent

	YEAR A	YEAR B	YEAR C
Genesis	12 : 1 - 4a	17 : 1 - 7, 15 - 16	15 : 1 - 12, 17 - 18
Psalm	121	22 : 23 - 31	27
Romans (A) / Romans (B) / Philippians (C)	4 : 1 - 5, 13 - 17	4 : 13 - 25	3 : 17- 4:1
St. John (A) / Mark (B) / St. Luke (C)	3 : 1 - 17	8 : 31 - 38	13 : 31 - 35

Third Sunday in Lent

	YEAR A	YEAR B	YEAR C
Exodus (A) / Exodus (B) / Isaiah (C)	17 : 1 - 7	20 : 1 - 17	55 : 1 - 9
Psalm	95	19	63 : 1 - 8
Romans (A) / 1 Corinthians (B) / 1 Corinthians (C)	5 : 1 - 11	1 : 18 - 25	10 : 1 - 13
St. John (A) / St. John (B) / St. Luke (C)	4 : 5 - 42	2 : 13 - 22	13 : 1 - 9

	YEAR A Beginning on the First Sunday of Advent in 1998, 2001, 2004, 2007, 2010, 2013, 2016	YEAR B Beginning on the First Sunday of Advent in 1999, 2002, 2005, 2008, 2011, 2014, 2017	YEAR C Beginning on the First Sunday of Advent in 2000, 2003, 2006, 2009, 2012, 2015, 2018
Fourth Sunday in Lent	1 Samuel 16 : 1 - 13 Psalm 23 Ephesians 5 : 8 - 14 St. John 9 : 1 - 41	Numbers 21 : 4 - 9 Psalm 107 : 1 - 3, 17 - 22 Ephesians 2 : 1 - 10 St. John 3 : 14 - 21	Joshua 5 : 9 - 12 Psalm 32 2 Corinthians 5 : 16 - 21 St. Luke 15 : 1 - 3, 11b - 32
Fifth Sunday in Lent	Ezekiel 37 : 1 - 14 Psalm 130 Romans 8 : 6 - 11 St. John 11 : 1 - 45	Jeremiah 31 : 31 - 34 Psalm 51 : 1 - 12 *or Psalm* 119: 9 - 16 Hebrews 5 : 5 - 10 St. John 12 : 20 - 33	Isaiah 43 : 16 - 21 Psalm 126 Philippians 3 : 4b - 14 St. John 12 : 1 - 8
HOLY WEEK	*Entry into J*	*Entry into J*	*Entry into J*
Sixth Sunday in Lent (Palm/Passion) *Whenever possible, even if readings for the Entry into Jerusalem are used, it is desirable that the complete Passion narrative should be read, as part of the preparation for Easter*	St. Matthew 21 : 1 - 11 Psalm 118 : 1 - 2, 19 - 26 *assion* P Isaiah 50 : 4 - 9a Psalm 31 : 9 - 16 Philippians 2 : 5 - 11 St. Matthew 26 :14 - 27:66 *or St. Matthew* 27 : 11 - 54	St. Mark 11 : 1 - 11 *or St. John* 12 : 12 - 16 Psalm 118: 1 - 2, 19 - 29 *assion* P Isaiah 50 : 4 - 9a Psalm 31 : 9 - 16 Philippians 2 : 5 - 11 St. Mark 14 : 1 - 15: 47 *or St. Mark* 15 : 1 - 39 (40 - 47)	St. Luke 19 : 28 - 40 Psalm 118 : 1 - 2, 19 - 29 *assion* P Isaiah 50 : 4 - 9a Psalm 31 : 9 - 16 Philippians 2 : 5 - 11 St. Luke 22 :14 - 23: 56 *or St. Luke* 23 : 1 - 49

	YEAR A Beginning on the First Sunday of Advent in 1998, 2001, 2004, 2007, 2010, 2013, 2016	YEAR B Beginning on the First Sunday of Advent in 1999, 2002, 2005, 2008, 2011, 2014, 2017	YEAR C Beginning on the First Sunday of Advent in 2000, 2003, 2006, 2009, 2012, 2015, 2018
Monday in Holy Week			
Isaiah	42 : 1 - 9	42 : 1 - 9	42 : 1 - 9
Psalm	36 : 5 - 11	36 : 5 - 11	36 : 5 - 11
Hebrews	9 : 11 - 15	9 : 11 - 15	9 : 11 - 15
St. John	12 : 1 - 11	12 : 1 - 11	12 : 1 - 11
Tuesday in Holy Week			
Isaiah	49 : 1 - 7	49 : 1 - 7	49 : 1 - 7
Psalm	71 : 1 - 14	71 : 1 - 14	71 : 1 - 14
1 Corinthians	1 : 18 - 31	1 : 18 - 31	1 : 18 - 31
St. John	12 : 20 - 36	12 : 20 - 36	12 : 20 - 36
Wednesday in Holy Week			
Isaiah	50 : 4 - 9a	50 : 4 - 9a	50 : 4 - 9a
Psalm	70	70	70
Hebrews	12 : 1 - 3	12 : 1 - 3	12 : 1 - 3
St. John	13 : 21 - 32	13 : 21 - 32	13 : 21 - 32
Thursday in Holy Week			
Exodus	12 : 1 - 14	12 : 1 - 14	12 : 1 - 14
Psalm	116 : 1 - 2, 12 - 19	116 : 1 - 2, 12 - 19	116 : 1 - 2, 12 - 19
1 Corinthians	11 : 23 - 26	11 : 23 - 26	11 : 23 - 26
St. John	13 : 1 - 17, 31b - 35	13 : 1 - 17, 31b - 35	13 : 1 - 17, 31b - 35

	YEAR A Beginning on the First Sunday of Advent in 1998, 2001, 2004, 2007, 2010, 2013, 2016	**YEAR B** Beginning on the First Sunday of Advent in 1999, 2002, 2005, 2008, 2011, 2014, 2017	**YEAR C** Beginning on the First Sunday of Advent in 2000, 2003, 2006, 2009, 2012, 2015, 2018
Good Friday			
Isaiah	52 : 13-53:12	52 : 13-53:12	52 : 13-53:12
Psalm	22	22	22
Hebrews	10 : 16 - 25	10 : 16 - 25	10 : 16 - 25
or Hebrews	4 : 14 - 16; 5 : 7 - 9	4 : 14 - 16; 5 : 7 - 9	4 : 14 - 16; 5 : 7 - 9
St. John	18 : 1 - 19: 42	18 : 1 - 19: 42	18 : 1 - 19: 42
Saturday *The pair including Ex* *These readings are for use at* *services other than an Easter Vigil.*			
Job	14 : 1 - 14	14 : 1 - 14	14 : 1 - 14
or Lamentations	3 : 1 - 9, 19 - 24	3 : 1 - 9, 19 - 24	3 : 1 - 9, 19 - 24
Psalm	31 : 1 - 4, 15 - 16	31 : 1 - 4, 15 - 16	31 : 1 - 4, 15 - 16
1 Peter	4 : 1 - 8	4 : 1 - 8	4 : 1 - 8
St. Matthew	27 : 57 - 66	27 : 57 - 66	27 : 57 - 66
or St. John	19 : 38 - 42	19 : 38 - 42	19 : 38 - 42
SEASON OF EASTER			
Resurrection of the Lord **Easter Vigil** *readings, together with* *an Epistle and a Gospel, should be*			
Genesis	1 : 1-2 : 4a	1 : 1-2 : 4a	1 : 1-2 : 4a
Psalm	136 : 1 - 9, 23 - 26	136 : 1 - 9, 23 - 26	136 : 1 - 9, 23 - 26
Genesis	7 : 1 - 5, 11 - 18; 8 : 6 - 18; 9 : 8 - 13	7 : 1 - 5, 11 - 18; 8 : 6 - 18; 9 : 8 - 13	7 : 1 - 5, 11 - 18; 8 : 6 - 18; 9 : 8 - 13
Psalm	46	46	46

YEAR A	YEAR B	YEAR C
Beginning on the First Sunday of Advent in 1998, 2001, 2004, 2007, 2010, 2013, 2016	Beginning on the First Sunday of Advent in 1999, 2002, 2005, 2008, 2011, 2014, 2017	Beginning on the First Sunday of Advent in 2000, 2003, 2006, 2009, 2012, 2015, 2018
Genesis 22 : 1 - 18	Genesis 22 : 1 - 18	Genesis 22 : 1 - 18
Psalm 16	Psalm 16	Psalm 16
Exodus 14 : 10 - 31; 15 : 20 - 21	Exodus 14 : 10 - 31; 15 : 20 - 21	Exodus 14 : 10 - 31; 15 : 20 - 21
Exodus 15 : 1b - 13, 17 - 18	Exodus 15 : 1b - 13, 17 - 18	Exodus 15 : 1b - 13, 17 - 18
Isaiah 55 : 1 - 11	Isaiah 55 : 1 - 11	Isaiah 55 : 1 - 11
Isaiah 12 : 2 - 6	Isaiah 12 : 2 - 6	Isaiah 12 : 2 - 6
Proverbs 8 : 1 - 8, 19 - 21; 9 : 4b - 6	Proverbs 8 : 1 - 8, 19 - 21; 9 : 4b - 6	Proverbs 8 : 1 - 8, 19 - 21; 9 : 4b - 6
Psalm 19	Psalm 19	Psalm 19
Ezekiel 36 : 24 - 28	Ezekiel 36 : 24 - 28	Ezekiel 36 : 24 - 28
Psalm 42 and 43	Psalm 42 and 43	Psalm 42 and 43
Ezekiel 37 : 1 - 4	Ezekiel 37 : 1 - 4	Ezekiel 37 : 1 - 4
Psalm 143	Psalm 143	Psalm 143
Zephaniah 3 : 14 - 20	Zephaniah 3 : 14 - 20	Zephaniah 3 : 14 - 20
Psalm 98	Psalm 98	Psalm 98
Romans 6 : 3 - 11	Romans 6 : 3 - 11	Romans 6 : 3 - 11
Psalm 114	Psalm 114	Psalm 114
St. Matthew 28 : 1 - 10	St. Mark 16 : 1 - 8	St. Luke 24 : 1 - 12

Easter Day

	YEAR A Beginning on the First Sunday of Advent in 1998, 2001, 2004, 2007, 2010, 2013, 2016	**YEAR B** Beginning on the First Sunday of Advent in 1999, 2002, 2005, 2003, 2011, 2014, 2017	**YEAR C** Beginning on the First Sunday of Advent in 2000, 2003, 2006, 2009, 2012, 2015, 2018
	Acts 10 : 34 - 43	Acts 10 : 34 - 43	Acts 10 : 34 - 43
	or Jeremiah 31 : 1 - 6	or Isaiah 25 : 6 - 9	or Isaiah 65 : 17 - 25
	Psalm 118 : 1 - 2, 14 - 24	Psalm 118 : 1 - 2, 14 - 24	Psalm 118 : 1 - 2, 14 - 24
	Colossians 3 : 1 - 4	1 Corinthians 15 : 1 - 11	1 Corinthians 15 : 19 - 26
	or Acts 10 : 34 - 43	or Acts 10 : 34 - 43	or Acts 10 : 34 - 43
	St. John 20 : 1 - 18	St. John 20 : 1 - 18	St. John 20 : 1 - 18
	or St. Matthew 28 : 1 - 10	or St. Mark 16 : 1 - 8	or St. Luke 24 : 1 - 12

Easter Evening

	YEAR A	**YEAR B**	**YEAR C**
	Isaiah 25 : 6 - 9	Isaiah 25 : 6 - 9	Isaiah 25 : 6 - 9
	Psalm 114	Psalm 114	Psalm 114
	1 Corinthians 5 : 6b - 8	1 Corinthians 5 : 6b - 8	1 Corinthians 5 : 6b - 8
	St. Luke 24 : 13 - 49	St. Luke 24 : 13 - 49	St. Luke 24 : 13 - 49

Second Sunday of Easter

	YEAR A	**YEAR B**	**YEAR C**
	Acts 2 : 14a, 22 - 32	Acts 4 : 32 - 35	Acts 5 : 27 - 32
	Psalm 16	Psalm 133	Psalm 118 : 14 - 29;
	or Exodus 15 : 1 - 11	or Isaiah 55 : 17 - 25	or Psalm 150
	Psalm 111	Psalm 3	or 2 Kings 7 : 1 - 16
			Psalm 2
	1 Peter 1 : 3 - 9	1 John 1 : 1 - 2 : 2	Revelation 1 : 4 - 8
	St. John 20 : 19 - 31	St. John 20 : 19 - 31	St. John 20 : 19 - 31

YEAR A — Beginning on the First Sunday of Advent in 1998, 2001, 2004, 2007, 2010, 2013, 2016

YEAR B — Beginning on the First Sunday of Advent in 1999, 2002, 2005, 2008, 2011, 2014, 2017

YEAR C — Beginning on the First Sunday of Advent in 2000, 2003, 2006, 2009, 2012, 2015, 2018

Third Sunday of Easter

	Year A	Year B	Year C
Acts	2 : 14a, 36 - 41	3 : 12 - 19	9 : 1 - 6, (7 - 20)
Psalm	116 : 1 - 4, 12 - 19	4	30
or Isaiah	51 : 1 - 6	6 : 1 - 9a	61 : 1 - 3
Psalm	34 : 1 - 10	40 : 1 - 5	90 : 13 - 17
1 Peter / 1 John / Revelation	1 Peter 1 : 17 - 23	1 John 3 : 1 - 7	Revelation 5 : 11 - 14
St. Luke / St. John	St. Luke 24 : 13 - 35	St. Luke 24 : 36b - 48	St. John 21 : 1 - 9

Fourth Sunday of Easter

	Year A	Year B	Year C
Acts	2 : 42 - 47	4 : 5 - 12	9 : 36 - 43
Psalm	23	23	23
or Ezekiel / Zechariah / Isaiah	Ezekiel 34 : 7 - 15	Zechariah 10	Isaiah 53 : 1 - 6
Psalm	100	80 : 1 - 7	114
1 Peter / 1 John / Revelation	1 Peter 2 : 19 - 25	1 John 3 : 16 - 24	Revelation 7 : 9 - 17
St. John	10 : 1 - 10	10 : 11 - 18	10 : 22 - 30

Fifth Sunday of Easter

	Year A	Year B	Year C
Acts	7 : 55 - 60	8 : 26 - 40	11 : 1 - 18
Psalm	31 : 1 - 5, 15 - 16	22 : 25 - 31	148
or Proverbs / Exodus / Leviticus	Proverbs 4 : 10 - 18	Exodus 19 : 1 - 6	Leviticus 19 : 9 - 18
Psalm	119 : 9 - 32	118 : 19 - 25	24 : 1 - 6
1 Peter / 1 John / Revelation	1 Peter 2 : 2 - 10	1 John 4 : 7 - 21	Revelation 21 : 1 - 6
St. John	14 : 1 - 14	15 : 1 - 8	13 : 31 - 35

	YEAR A Beginning on the First Sunday of Advent in 1998, 2001, 2004, 2007, 2010, 2013, 2016	**YEAR B** Beginning on the First Sunday of Advent in 1999, 2002, 2005, 2008, 2011, 2014, 2017	**YEAR C** Beginning on the First Sunday of Advent in 2000, 2003, 2006, 2009, 2012, 2015, 2018
Sixth Sunday of Easter	Acts 17 : 22 - 31 Psalm 66 : 8 - 20 or Ezekiel 43 : 1 - 7a Psalm 115 1 Peter 3 : 13 - 22 St. John 14 : 15 - 21	Acts 10 : 44 - 48 Psalm 98 : or Genesis 35 : 9 - 15 Psalm 101 1 John 5 : 1 - 6 St. John 15 : 9 - 17	Acts 16 : 9 - 15 Psalm 67 or Deuteronomy 34 : 1 - 12 Psalm 109 : 21 - 31 Revelation 21 :10,22-22:5 St. John 14 : 23 - 29 or St. John 5 : 1 - 9
Ascension of the Lord These readings may also be used on the Seventh Sunday of Easter.	Acts 1 : 1 - 11 Psalm 47 or 93 or Danie 7 : 9 - 14 Psalm 24 : 7 - 10 Ephesians 1 : 15 - 23 St. Luke 24 : 44 - 53	Acts 1 : 1 - 11 Psalm 47 or 93 or Daniel 7 : 9 - 14 Psalm 68 : 15 - 20, 32 - 35 Ephesians 1 : 15 - 23 St. Luke 24 : 44 - 53	Acts 1 : 1 - 11 Psalm 47 or 93 or Daniel 7 : 9 - 14 Psalm 113 Ephesians 1 : 15 - 23 St. Luke 24 : 44 - 53
Seventh Sunday of Easter	Acts 1 : 6 - 14 Psalm 68 : 1 - 10, 32 - 35 or Isaiah 45 : 1 - 7 Psalm 21 : 1 - 7, 1 Peter 4 : 12 - 14; 5 : 6 - 11 St. John 17 : 1 - 11	Acts 1 : 15 - 17, 21 - 26 Psalm 1 or Jeremiah 10 : 1 - 10a Psalm 108 1 John 5 : 9 - 13 St. John 17 : 6 - 19	Acts 16 : 16 - 34 Psalm 97 or 2 Kings 2 : 1 - 15 Psalm 2 Revelation 22 : 12 -14, 16-17,20-21 St. John 17 : 20 - 26

Index of first lines

*The character or speaker is indicated after each first line. For **scripts** or **readings** where the first line is that of the narrator (and which may, in any case, be optional), the first line of the next character or speaker is also given.*

The Wild Goose Resource & Worship Groups

The **Wild Goose Resource Group** is an expression of the Iona Community's commitment to the renewal of public worship. Based in Glasgow, the Group has four members (Alison Adam, John Bell, Graham Maule and Mairi Munro) who are employed full-time and who lead workshops and seminars throughout Britain and abroad.

The WGRG's sister group, the **Wild Goose Worship Group** (to which the four WGRG workers also belong), consists of sixteen members who represent a variety of occupations and denominations.

Both groups are engaged in developing and identifying new methods and materials to enable the revitalization of congregational song, prayer and liturgy. The songs and liturgical material are frequently broadcast on radio and television.

The WGRG publishes a twice-yearly newsletter, **Goose***Gander,* to enable friends and supporters to keep abreast of WGWG and WGRG developments.

The Iona Community

The Iona Community is an ecumenical Christian community, founded in 1938 by the late Lord MacLeod of Fuinary (the Revd George MacLeod DD) and committed to seeking new ways of living the Gospel in today's world. Gathered around the rebuilding of the ancient monastic buildings of Iona Abbey, but with its original inspiration in the poorest areas of Glasgow during the Depression, the Community has sought ever since the "rebuilding of the common life," bringing together work and worship, prayer and politics, the sacred and the secular in ways that reflect its strongly incarnational theology.

The Community today is a movement of some 200 members, over 1,400 associate members and about 1,600 friends. The members — women and men from many backgrounds and denominations, most in Britain, but some overseas — are committed to a rule of daily prayer and Bible reading, sharing and accounting for their use of time and money, regular meeting and action for justice and peace.

The Iona Community maintains three centers on Iona and Mull: Iona Abbey and the MacLeod Centre on Iona, and Camas Adventure Camp on the Ross of Mull. Its base is in Community House, Glasgow, where it also supports work with young people, the Wild Goose Resource and Worship Groups, a bimonthly magazine (*Coracle*) and a publishing house (Wild Goose Publications).

For further information on the Iona Community please contact:
The Iona Community
Pearce Institute,
840 Govan Road
Glasgow G51 3UU
Tel. U.K.: 141 445 4561; **Fax U.K.:** 141 445 4295
e-mail: ionacomm@gla.iona.org.uk